"When it comes to decisions about dating, teenagers are in a serious crisis. They are bombarded with all kinds of mixed and mixed-up messages about sex and sexuality. The results of poor decision making in these realms of their lives not only impact their relationships for the rest of their lives but also can result in devastating physical and emotional consequences. Andy takes the issues surrounding dating and sexuality head-on to help you as a parent understand not only what your teen is going through, being taught, and thinking but also how to talk with your teen within the context of a biblical worldview. Thanks, Andy, for another honest and practical book on our teens and the culture that seeks to devour them."

—WALT LARIMORE, MD, author of *God's Design for the Highly Healthy Teen*

"As a Bible teacher seeking to integrate God's Word into teenagers' lives each day, I've found that the topic of teen sex and dating has been grossly ignored or ignorantly engaged. The heartbreaking reality is that my students are bearing the consequences of the lack of biblical insight in this area, and the consequences are long-lasting. I am very excited that Andy Braner is writing on this topic, as I trust him to deliver God's truth to our kids."

—JAY MENDENHALL, Bible teacher, Oklahoma Bible Academy, Enid, Oklahoma

"Andy Braner hits it out of the park with this one—a must-read for parents who care about what their teen or preteen is doing and thinking. The approach is straightforward and fresh, with no stone unturned. I blushed a few times but couldn't put it down. Read it and you will be shocked. Don't read it and the consequences may be far worse."

—CARL MEDEARIS, Middle East peace catalyst; author of *Muslims, Christians, and Jesus, Speaking of Jesus,* and *Tea with Hezbollah* (with Ted Dekker)

"This book fills such a need. Our youth have bought the lie that sex is simply a physical function much like exercise that needs to be practiced and expertise developed. Our generation has failed to communicate how sex is a precious gift that needs to be properly cared for. As with any gift from God, the use of it needs to please Him!"

—ROSEMARY MEHAN, Bible study teacher, Valley Christian High School, Chandler, Arizona

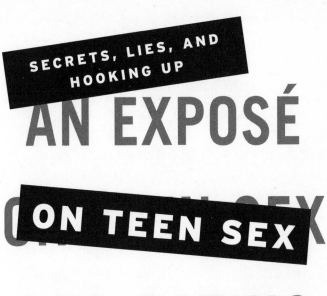

SECRETS, LIES, AND
HOOKING UP

AN EXPOSÉ

ON TEEN SEX

AND DATING

**WHAT'S REALLY GOING ON AND HOW TO
TALK ABOUT IT**

ANDY BRANER

NAVPRESS

Discipleship Inside Out™

Discipleship Inside Out™

NavPress is the publishing ministry of The Navigators, an international Christian organization and leader in personal spiritual development. NavPress is committed to helping people grow spiritually and enjoy lives of meaning and hope through personal and group resources that are biblically rooted, culturally relevant, and highly practical.

For a free catalog go to www.NavPress.com
or call 1.800.366.7788 in the United States or 1.800.839.4769 in Canada.

ISBN-13: 978-1-61521-923-0

Cover Design: Faceout Studio, Jason Gabbert

Some of the anecdotal illustrations in this book are true to life and are included with the permission of the persons involved. All other illustrations are composites of real situations, and any resemblance to people living or dead is coincidental.

Unless otherwise identified, all Scripture quotations in this publication are taken from the *Holy Bible, New International Version*® (NIV®). Copyright © 1973, 1978, 1984 by International Bible Society. Used by permission of Zondervan. All rights reserved. Other versions used include: the New King James Version (NKJV). Copyright © 1982 by Thomas Nelson, Inc. Used by permission. All rights reserved; *THE MESSAGE* (MSG). Copyright © 1993, 1994, 1995, 1996, 2000, 2001, 2002. Used by permission of NavPress Publishing Group; the *Holy Bible*, New Living Translation (NLT), copyright © 1996, 2004. Used by permission of Tyndale House Publishers, Inc., Wheaton, Illinois 60189. All rights reserved; and the King James Version (KJV).

Library of Congress Cataloging-in-Publication Data

Braner, Andy.

An exposé on teen sex and dating : what's really going on and how to talk about it / Andy Braner.

p. cm.

Includes bibliographical references.

ISBN 978-1-61521-923-0

1. Sexual ethics for teenagers. 2. Interpersonal relations in adolescence. 3. Dating (Social customs) I. Title.

HQ35.B8135 2011

241'.6765--dc22

2010050548

Printed in the United States of America

1 2 3 4 5 6 7 8 / 16 15 14 13 12 11

I dedicate this book to the parents and youth leaders helping to raise our teenagers, and to the teenagers who are navigating the hardest sexual culture ever on the planet. I hope this book helps.

Download a free discussion guide at
www.NavPress.com.

CONTENTS

ACKNOWLEDGMENTS

I'D LIKE TO say thanks to all the folks at NavPress. Thanks to Rebekah, Kris, and all the publishing people who helped make this book possible. Thanks to Amy Parker for her relentless work editing and getting this book to sound just right. Thanks to all my staff at KIVU: Luke, Tamara, Mike, Susan, Bob, and Julie—you guys are the greatest. Thanks to all the college students who helped put the stories into context for college kids. Thanks to the teenagers interviewed; you guys were great! Thanks for being open and honest with me through the process. I hope we can change the course of history. Thanks to my family: Braner Party of 7, you guys ROCK! Jamie Jo, you're my best friend, my love, my life. And finally, thanks be to God for the great things He has done, is doing, and will do. To Him be all the glory!

INTRODUCTION

REMEMBER WHEN DATING was a hamburger and a movie?

What about the occasional trip to the mall, where boys and girls followed each other around with puppy dog eyes, ogling at one another? Remember doing that?

Remember homecoming games where girls wore letter jackets to show the world they were thinking about a relationship a bit more serious than just friends?

Well, to put it bluntly, those days are over.

I've been around teenagers most of my life. Starting as a small kid mentored in youth group at my local church to actually leading the group, I've experienced and viewed teenage life from many different angles. I've been doing youth ministry for more than fifteen years, and I've invested my life in knowing and learning what teenagers do, why they do those things, and how we as parents and leaders can help them grow up and make wise choices in a hostile world.

My wife and I run a camp for teens in Colorado. Each summer we see a thousand teenagers from all over the globe who are interested in knowing what they believe and why they believe it. We offer a real-life Colorado adventure for teens and give them the opportunity to ask tough questions about life. To date, we've seen almost ten thousand students at our summer camp. My "off season" is filled with speaking requests, spiritual emphasis weeks, and weekend retreats for churches, schools, and other organizations, speaking to teens, parents, and youth leaders.

This book is something I've thought about writing for a long time. I knew this book needed to be written, but the effects of what I've penned here have far-reaching consequences.

You see, up until now, I've been a "cool" teen-friendly guy. I've been able to hang with teenagers, talk about their innermost struggles, and walk with them through hard times. But I'm risking it all to let you know: WE MUST DO SOMETHING FAST!

I'm willing to risk my reputation as the cool guy so we can put our minds together and help teens walk through this dating stuff. And let's be honest: If you're like me, our dating history is far from perfect and holy, but as I've interviewed hundreds of teens concerning dating relationships in their world, I've learned that what's going on in the hallways of today's high schools would make the marginal eighties dater blush. Not only is there a plague of teenage sexuality, a rise in STDs among teens, and a lack of intimate relationships with high school students, but *teens want help*. In fact, the number one question asked of me by teenagers centers around relationships and how they interact with one another.

They're searching for ways to answer questions like:

- How do guys relate to girls?
- How do girls relate to guys?
- How far is too far in a physical relationship?
- Is it okay to date?
- How do I date?
- What do I *do* on a date?

And do you know where they're finding answers?

- Hollywood
- The hip-hop community
- Television sitcoms and reality shows
- Their friends

Now don't get me wrong, but this is a little like the blind leading the blind.

We must be a society that helps our teens and students understand the importance of relating to each other in the real world — and no, not MTV's version — or we will continue watching the state of the union degrade to a cesspool of sexuality. I don't know if you're aware or not, but according to Jennifer Parker of *Christianity Today* in a recent article concerning the sex lives of Christian teens, Christian high school students are having sex, and subsequently having babies, as much as or even more than non-Christian students.

On a recent trip to southern Arizona, I asked a prominent ear, nose, and throat doctor about the most-addressed issue he sees in his practice. Do you know what he told me? Syphilis of the mouth.

Syphilis of the mouth?!

What in the world is going on in our culture when a doctor's practice becomes inundated with syphilis of the mouth more than something like strep throat or a normal seasonal flu?

Truth be told, sexually transmitted diseases are as high among Christians today as they are among nonbelievers, and in some demographics, they're even higher among Christians.

Now wait a minute . . .

If we are people who believe in God . . .

If we are people who believe in obeying God's commandments . . .

What in the world is going on?

Why are high school students drowning in a sea of sexuality with no end in sight?

Every time I speak to a group of teens, I make sure to get away from the mainstream for a bit. I take groups of anywhere from five to fifty students aside and start asking questions about what's going on in the dating scene today. Their answers, when they're being honest, would make your toes curl. They've shared stories with me that were X-rated movies in the eighties. And it's even happening in the classroom. *Literally in the classroom.*

Schools today are more like cesspools of sexuality than centers of learning. Some teens are having sex *in class*. I recently heard a story from a young girl who told me she watched a boyfriend/girlfriend duo actually have sex when the biology teacher darkened the lights to show a movie in class.

What is happening to our teens?

Where do they get the idea that hormones should dictate their behavioral choices?

I've written quite a bit about belief systems and the effects on behavior, but this is at a whole new level.

Many people think dating in the twenty-first century is just like dating was back when we were in high school, but nothing could be further from the truth. The days of going to dinner and a movie, with images of a boy opening the car door for a girl and a girl sitting properly and waiting on the boy's initiation — please hear me loud and clear — *those days are over!* If we continue thinking about dating in the context of our own experiences, we're going to watch a generation struggle through sexual depression and emotional guilt, and consequences that may last a lifetime. Dating in today's world has taken a turn and, if not addressed, will continue to slide to an uncontrollable level of decadence.

We can't turn our eyes away any longer and pretend nothing is happening.

We can't assume our teenagers are committing themselves to courtship anymore.

This could be the greatest issue concerning Christian teens going forward, and it can have the most impact from an emotional, physical, and certainly a sexual point of view.

WE MUST ACT NOW!

It's time we lay aside the weirdness of talking about sex.

It's time to be honest with our kids.

We need to talk about desire, defeat, and demoralization.

We need to give teens the choice to make decisions in light of the consequences.

We need more mentors.

We need more people who care about the physical, emotional, and spiritual well-being of our teens rather than how many certificates were handed out at the local purity rally.

You can use this book as a study guide, a reference book, or even a devotional book at your local church. My goal is to help parents and those working with teenagers walk students through the most confusing time of their lives. With hormones blazing and sexuality being sold at every single turn, teens need a place where they can ask hard questions—and get some answers.

I'm no Dr. Love. (Just ask my wife.) But I can offer an interesting look into the world of teenage dating, and I want to expose what's going on in the hallways of our high schools so we can come to some sort of plan to help our teens.

I believe in teenagers.

I believe in dating.

I believe in relationships.

I believe God created men and women for specific purposes.

I believe there are hormones.

I believe there is desire.

I believe there are needs that must be met in a relationship.

As we begin to outline the purpose of dating . . .

I believe teenagers can date.

I refuse to believe they are just sex-crazed animals.

I refuse to believe we have to go back to the arranged marriages of old.

I refuse to believe we must "kiss dating goodbye."

In fact . . .

I believe dating, if used well, can be a wonderful tool to help teens grow into a marriage relationship.

I believe dating can help teens contextualize the world around them with their peers.

I believe the concept of dating can lead to lifelong friendships.

But we've got to start helping our kids know the boundaries.

We've got to ask them the tough questions and provide the tough answers.

We've got to be committed to sexual purity, emotional stability, and spiritual maturity.

I start by asking teens questions like these:

- Why do we date?
- Is dating important?
- What social growth happens when a guy and girl date?
- What is God's view of dating?
- When should teens start dating?
- How should teens date?
- What can we consider "too far" physically?
- Can teens really date in the confines of God's kingdom on earth?

I hope to answer these questions—and many more—throughout this book. I pray that as we are a people who seek first His kingdom and His righteousness, all of these things will be given to us (see Matthew 6:33).

I believe there are some relevant truths inside this strange cultural dance called dating. And I do believe we have a responsibility to teach teens how to dance in this arena.

So, if you don't believe in dating . . .

If you think dating is an abomination . . .

If you don't think there's any point to even talking about dating . . .

Or if you're a parent or leader who doesn't think your teen would ever get involved in this stuff . . .

This isn't the book for you.

But if you'd like an insider's look at what's really going on at the dances . . .

If you want to read what teens are telling me about the parties . . .

If you'd like to be a part of the change in cultural understanding . . .

Then don't put this book down.

I believe, if given the right tools, our teenagers can rise up to be the next great generation.

I believe if we stop living life *at* them and start living *with* them . . .

Together, we can welcome them into this wonderful relational dance between a man and a woman. We will see marriages restored, sexual issues begin to fade away, and young men and women committing the whole of their sexuality to the One who created them.

We don't need more guilt.

We don't need teens to sign marriage covenants, as some counselors believe will help curb the divorce rates. We've already committed, right?

We don't need to focus on purity parties (although I do think awareness is a crucial component).

We need to help teenagers walk through a rite of passage.

Teens need to be able to seriously look at the advantages of dating and cognitively see the disadvantages.

I believe if we begin to paint a godly picture of a relationship between a man and a woman, teens who want to follow Jesus will respond. They'll want to see it done right and successfully.

This book is dedicated to helping those who are walking in the dark shadows of high school, longing to talk with someone about relationships. My hope is that through the next few chapters, you'll be inspired to talk with your teens and the students in your sphere of influence and help them navigate the hardest issues in growing up. We are all sexual people, and we need to take a serious look at helping kids understand ways they can express their sexuality inside of God's ultimate plan for their lives.

They're tired of divorce, cheating, and the sick, perverse way the media is telling them to date. In fact, I believe teenagers know in their heart of hearts what it means to have a successful dating relationship. Unfortunately, the world they live in doesn't allow them to stand up for what they believe.

Here's their story.

Straight from their mouths.

My prayer is that . . .

We will be a culture strong enough to face tough issues.

We will see reality without turning our heads.

We will confront those realities and help find answers for teenagers who are emotionally dying to know how to love.

I offer an invitation to you, just as I to do the teenagers whom I disciple: "Let's talk."

PART I

A VIEW OF DATING

CHAPTER 1

IS DATING EVEN IN THE BIBLE?

CONTRARY TO COMMON youth-group discussions, I can't find dating *anywhere* in the Bible.

There's no handbook on relationships in the New Testament.

There's no step-by-step process to teach us how to enter into a relationship.

There's not even a good understanding of how to accomplish the courting model anywhere.

The reason is simple.

Back in biblical times, there was no such thing as dating. They didn't even have anything called courtship. The truth, plain and simple, is that one family betrothed a woman to a young man in another family, and the marriage was arranged. It was that easy. Parents decided whom their children were going to marry, sometimes from the moment they were born. I ask teenagers around the world, "Do you want to go back to the days of arranged marriages?" And they answer with a resounding "No!" We have to find another way.

Without a spiritual guidebook for dating, we need to figure out if God intended there to be a "dating" relationship, and if so, how we can help educate, encourage, and mentor those who will be dating.

One thing I do know: Teens aren't going to revert back to the golden years.

They're always looking for the newest, latest, greatest something that's going on in the world. And if that something meets the needs they're feeling at the time, they'll jump on it, and they'll jump *fast*.

So, this leads us to an odd conundrum: How can we date from a biblical model if dating isn't even in there?

It doesn't take long for the story of marriage to be clearly seen in the Old Testament. From Adam and Eve in Genesis 2 to Noah and his wife and their three sons and wives in Genesis 9, it is clear relationships were engineered to be one man and one woman for life. But what about dating? How do we get from an archaic system of family arrangements to a modern way of thinking? Did we miss something? Are we engaged in a practice God didn't intend?

GUIDELINES FOR DATING . . . AND BEYOND

In order to understand this practice of knowing each other, we've got to look at some basic concepts. Remember, the Bible wasn't written in a way that you can always mirror your life after the stories there. Rather, it was written so we can learn tenets of God's law, His best practices, and apply them to a culture that exists outside biblical times.

#1: God is always involved.

One lesson clearly highlighted in relationships from biblical days is the fact that God is always in the middle of setting up romance. Adam could no more have found Eve without God than Samson could have worked out to get stronger on his own. God is *always* involved. Acceptance and application of this one fact would have simplifying effects reaching from the dating world all the way into the biology classrooms of the universities. God sees, knows, and orchestrates even the tiniest details of our lives.

Imagine how hard it is to find your one mate out of the seven billion people living on this planet. As adults, we know the pitfalls of dating, the countless years it takes to hone in on what you want in a mate, and the testing and trials it takes before you know you've found the one you want to be with.

Imagine if there were no humans on the planet. It would be impossible to find a male and a female ready to engage in a marriage relationship without another human being on the planet! If evolution of humanity is true, then the miracle for the right man and the right woman to find each other at just the right time is almost as big of a miracle as if God had created them male and female as He described in Genesis 1:27.

As we teach teens how to understand God's will in terms of their dating life, we must continue to work out the theology of God's sovereignty. There is a plan. I believe God has known our days (see Psalm 139:16), made His will known (see Romans 12:2), and given us freedom to follow Him (see Luke 9:23). It works in the big issues of vocation and education as much as it works in the issues of relationships. I believe God has ordained certain relationships to happen in His timing.

#2: God's plan is perfect, but often His timing is strange.

Remember the story of Abraham and Sarah? God promised Abraham that he would be the father of many nations. Abraham was going to have a son, and through that son, God was going to establish a new generation of people who were going to follow Him. In Genesis 18 Sarah laughed at God as she realized she was too old to have a child, let alone raise this child God had promised her. But it wasn't long before Isaac was born, at just the right time (see Genesis 21). Even though Abraham was one hundred years old and Sarah was ninety, God's timing was perfect for them to have a son. Strange? Maybe. But perfect nonetheless.

Sometimes I think teenagers (and beyond!) rush into relationships because they want to preempt God's timing. Some girls think they'll never get married unless they marry the man standing before them right then. Some guys get caught up in the physical attraction and are willing to rush into incompatible commitments. But God's timing can't be regulated to what makes sense in the moment. After all, Abraham had a child at *one hundred*. That just isn't possible. Right? That's true, until God gets involved. (See #1.)

As we teach teens and students about God's timing, it's important not to set up any sort of unrealistic expectations. Sometimes it will happen in accordance with our plans, but if God is behind it, guiding and directing, you can't merely rely on the wisdom of tradition. God's ways are certainly higher than our ways, and His plans are higher than ours (see Isaiah 55:9). We may not always understand His plans, but if we try to seek His will, we'll more likely be in accordance with those plans.

#3: Some just aren't ready.

It really is my intent to help shape the way teenagers date today. I believe dating can be a useful tool in understanding members of the opposite sex. I think male-to-female communication can be a valuable resource in figuring out how to navigate the turgid waters of marriage and relationships in the future. But to be honest, in my search to redefine dating, I can't in good conscience say that it is the right time for everyone to date.

There are certain times when it's going to be right to date, and other times when we'll have to teach kids how to recognize their illiteracy when it comes to dating. Girls need to understand the dangers of sharing their emotional life with someone. Guys need to understand that dating isn't about just trying to "hook up" with a girl. Girls need to know guys have feelings too. Guys need to recognize the massive responsibility they are taking on when they decide to care for a girl's heart in the context of a relationship.

Sometimes, no matter how old or how mature kids think they are, it's good to step back and admit that dating isn't for everyone. In a general sense, however, I'm going to do everything I can to educate parents and leaders on the world of dating today and how to best approach it.

THE DATING SURVEY

I travel all over the world trying to help teenagers understand how to incorporate biblical principles into everyday life, and dating is the big question.

Should we date?

How old do we have to be to date?

How do we know we're in love?

How far is too far (physically)?

I start every session with a simple question: "Why do we date?" And you should see the hands go up.

"Because we want to have fun."

"So we can hang out."

"We like girls," say the guys.

"We want a free meal," say the girls.

The list can fill a dry-erase board twelve feet long with answers to promote dating in their own way.

They know *why* they date, but often they're afraid to admit the real reason.

After we line out all the answers they come up with, I try to clarify the situation a bit. "Come on, let's be honest. There's no reason to make up answers that sound so vanilla." And I shout out, "Why do we date? I mean, what's the difference between a friend that's a boy, and a boyfriend?" Eventually the real answers start pouring forth.

"*We like to make out!*" they scream.

Okay, so now we're being honest.

You see, the current thought on dating in high school is:

- A boyfriend is someone who can give me physical attention.
- A girlfriend is someone who can satisfy my hormonal urges.
- A boyfriend will continue being my boyfriend as long as I give him something physically.
- A girlfriend is someone I can count on when I need a physical release.

Now I know this sounds stereotypical, but the majority of teenagers I talk with can categorize their dating relationships in these terms. While they would rather not be called boyfriend and girlfriend, they see a relationship with someone of the opposite sex as opportunistic. It has nothing to do with commitment and everything to do with pleasure.

One boy told me, "At my school, when there is a dance coming up, a guy will text a girl to 'hook up.' [This is code for, 'Let's make out.'] When they hook up, if everything goes as planned and they seem to like each other, then they might go to the dance together. It's all about how much they can do physically."

One girl told me, "At my school it's just understood that you have two weeks. You start hooking up, making out, having sex, and everyone knows that in two weeks it will be over and you move on to someone else."

It's almost like they see relationships as an amusement park. There are lots of roller coasters to ride, so I'll just ride this one until it gets boring or it's obviously over, and then it's on to a new one. Dating becomes something of an instant gratifier to match our culture. Let's just admit it: *We don't like to wait on anything.*

We have drive-through meals.

We have coffee in an instant.

We have microwaves to make food for us in seconds.

And we want relationships to be all or nothing in an instant. But guess what? That's not how God designed it. Even in marriage, there is a journey of relationship. Sometimes it's really good, and sometimes it can be difficult. There's no reason dating should be any different. Just because teenagers are out dating doesn't mean they have to jump from getting to know each other to an instant physical relationship. There is a process. There are stages. There is something about a progressive relationship that makes it rich and sweet. If we can teach teenagers that relationships aren't about instant gratification, then maybe we can begin curbing some of these instant physical relationships.

I recently spoke to a teenager in a large public high school. She told me the classification for dating now is to point at a boy and a girl and label them, "They've got a thing." A "thing" is just that, a moment in time where they had something beyond a friendship, often a culmination of some sort of physical desire. The strange part about this story is not the new label; we've been creating new labels for relationships for a long time. No, the strange part about this relationship is the lack of guilt and commitment the two felt when they came back to school the next day. A "thing" might be something of a torrid physical lovefest on Monday night, but Tuesday in the hallway of the high school, that's all it was. It was a moment when two people got together, and neither holds any sort of commitment to the event whatsoever.

These stories could be told a thousand times over. Most teenagers aren't dating; they're just trying to see how far they can go with anyone who's willing. Seriously, the whole idea of dating has turned into a cesspool of physical relationships.

Let me be straight here: If this is what dating is, then I'm solely against it. The Bible talks about sexual immorality almost as much as it talks about how to enter the kingdom of heaven. It's a real deal to God.

Ephesians 5:3 says, "Among you there must not be even a hint of sexual immorality." If that's the case, and we want to teach teenagers how to date, then we've got to start training them concerning the importance of dating. Otherwise they're going to learn from every movie star, TV actor, and celebrity they see.

They need to learn what the purpose of dating really is:

- It's not about getting married.
- It's not about going steady.
- It's not about whatever physical act they can get or give to each other.

Dating has to be about helping students understand the process of knowing.

They need to learn what it means to *know* someone else and to *be known* by someone.

The worst way to teach them is to just stand up in front and preach the message, "God wants you to wait until you get married."

Because we've tried that.

It doesn't work.

Just look at the statistics of Christian marriages that are failing. They're almost right in line with non-Christian marriages, according to research by the Barna Group.[1] And Christians have all the marriage counselors in the world.

So what's the problem?

We've got abstinence programs.

We've got purity rallies.

We've got courtship.

We've got group dating.

We've got the Bible, which speaks directly to sexual immorality, yet the dating practices of Christian teenagers are *the same* as non-Christians.

Girls are still getting pregnant.

STDs are still running rampant.

And the emotional trauma happening to our teenagers is almost criminal.

I was in a small group of teenagers not long ago, and one girl told me that in her Christian high school "at least 80 percent of the students are having sex."

"No way! Eighty percent?" I asked.

"Absolutely. There's just nothing wrong with it in my school."

NOTHING WRONG?

What about the emotional trauma brought on by sharing your body with someone who will inherently break up with you?

What about the chance of physical disease?

What about the spiritual understanding that God made one man for one woman?

What about the guilt you're going to carry with you into your marriage?

What about the conversation you'll have with your future mate?

What about the passing on of dating practices to your children?

These questions need to be asked and addressed. *Teenagers need to understand the significance of sexuality.* They watch the latest TV show or celebrity relationship, and they're only exposed to the good aspects of relationships and sex. The star of the movie always ends up with the girl. That's the way fairy tales go. But Hollywood never shows the aftereffects when the star runs out on the girl to date someone else. It never shows the issues running around in the minds of teenagers as they try to navigate other relationships. It paints an unrealistic picture of relationships, and our teens are listening.

So when teens—at Christian high schools, no less—merely think there's "nothing wrong" with sharing your physical body with someone else outside the confines of marriage, we as parents and leaders have a pretty big hill to climb.

It's time we reframe the purpose for dating.

It's time we nail down some dos and don'ts for our kids.

It's time we help them, rather than turning a blind eye to the issues out there.

We need to be clear with our kids when it comes to sexuality.

We need not fear our own pasts for the sake of the next generation. In fact, sometimes our past failures can serve as the best lessons for students heading for a world filled with disappointing sexual experiences.

We need to understand that the teenage world today is barraged with sexual promises, dreams of romantic bliss, and inconsequential decisions; it's our responsibility to help guide them to healthy relationships.

And I think I can help.

THE PURPOSE OF RELATIONSHIPS

Even though the Bible doesn't speak clearly on dating, I do believe we can extrapolate some common relational themes to begin building a case for students. After all, if we want them to be successful in their teenage years and grow to be people who have successful families, we owe it to them.

The Bible is clear about the purpose for relationships.

It all started back in Genesis chapter 2.

When God put Adam in the garden, He was about to give him the job of naming all the animals. Can you imagine?

The God of the universe just created all the stuff we see in the galaxies. He put the dew on the flowers and spun Jupiter on its orbit. He caused the ecosystems of the earth to function well with one another, and He orchestrated the cosmic wonders like black holes, neutron stars, and supernovae.

And here He stands, ready to hand over one of the most

important parts of naming creation to this man named Adam.

Right before the ceremony was to begin, God said, "It is not good for the man to be alone. I will make a helper suitable for him" (verse 18).

Reason #1: To Experience True Companionship

Have you ever found yourself truly alone? I don't mean alone like when you walked through the hallways of school and felt like you didn't know anyone. I mean, have you ever been in a place where you closed the door at night, and all around you it was just you and God?

It's a scary thing to think that you might find yourself alone in the world.

I was recently in Saint Louis at a national youth convention. It's one of those Christian events to bring youth leaders in from around the world. They have concerts, speakers, and a long hallway of sponsors trying to sell the latest Christian products. I know there is a place for all that stuff. But sometimes I just need to go be with people who think differently than I do. I decided to go outside the convention center and walk the streets of Saint Louis to see what I could run into.

As I started walking downtown, the sky was dark, cars were buzzing all around me, and there seemed to be plenty of activity going on, but I started feeling a little bit lonely. Even though there were tons of people around, I experienced a lack of "knowing" at that very moment.

"Hey, buddy, can I bum some change off you?" A man stretched out his hand.

"Hey, how are you?"

"I'm doing okay, just a bit hungry tonight. Think you can spare some cash for me, buddy?"

"I tell you what: Why don't we go down to the local Chili's, and I'll buy you something to eat?"

I know it probably wasn't the smartest move in the world. How many stories have you heard where someone trying to do something good is caught in a compromising situation? I understand that. But at this particular moment, I needed to talk. I needed to share something with somebody. As much as this guy needed something to eat, I needed someone I could share life with for a while.

It didn't take long before I learned how this guy got to the streets of Saint Louis. He told me how he was living under one of the bridges and how his girlfriend broke up with him; he lost his job and was trying to get back on his feet.

We sat at Chili's for an hour or so: He got a belly full of baby back ribs, while I got a much-needed relational fill. It was strange. As much as he needed the food, I needed the friendship.

It's funny how God made us that way. He saw that man needed to be with someone. He knew that over the course of a lifetime, Adam couldn't have survived on his own. Crazy as it may sound, think of it like this . . .

God walked in the garden.

Adam walked in the garden.

God said, "It isn't good that man be alone!"

Now, what can we make of that statement?

Was Adam truly alone?

NO . . .

He had GOD!

He walked with God.

He talked with God.

He laughed with God.

He shared all the cool stories of the day with the Creator of the heavens and the earth.

Yet . . . God understood. He saw it necessary that man not walk on the earth void of humanity. We were created to be together.

To laugh together.

To weep together.

To rejoice together.

To share life together.

Adam needed Eve for companionship.

And soon we'll find out, Eve needed Adam too.

Loneliness—that need for companionship—is the primary issue teenagers are dealing with today. Whether it's the friends they choose to hang out with or the boyfriend or girlfriend they choose to date, the loneliness that God created inside the heart of mankind from the very beginning is the issue that needs to be dealt with.

Not long ago, one of my mentors had a telling conversation with a girl at a local high school.

"Hey, Audry, how are you?" he asked.

"I'm not doing well."

"What seems to be bothering you?" he asked as they sat at the top of the bleachers and looked down at the Friday night football game being played on the luscious green grass.

"See all those kids down there? They all have it together. They all have a life. I feel like I'm the only one that struggles through life and wonders about whether I should go to college, who I should marry, and what I should do with my life."

"Oh, Audry. Can I offer a bit of advice?" he offered empathetically.

"Sure, you always make me feel better."

"You are a beautiful young lady," he commented as he collected his thoughts.

"Thank you."

"You're on the cheer team."

"Yeah."

"You're the captain, right?"

"Uh-huh."

"If you—this beautiful young lady, captain of the cheer squad, friends with almost everyone in the school—are feeling alone, what do you think the rest of those kids are feeling?"

"Oh. I didn't ever look at it like that."

"You're not alone, my friend. Everyone has the same need for togetherness in his or her heart. Some fill it with production. Some with alcohol. Still others with drugs and sex. But the issue is the same: We all need each other in some way."

And that was it.

Audry realized for the first time in her life that loneliness is a shared component of the human existence.

If we're honest with ourselves, we'll admit that most of the dating disaster plaguing our culture today comes from an appetite of togetherness misguided, misunderstood, and misplaced in an emotional sphere disconnected from God's original intention. Teenagers are walking through the hallways of high school with *plenty* of people around. They can reach out with the latest smart phones and Twitter or Facebook to any number of thousands of friends, yet they feel like I did when I was walking down the streets of Saint Louis. They need to be "with" someone — face to face, heart to heart.

The problem is, the only place we've allowed it to happen, and maybe even forced it to happen, is within the context of dating. Teenagers see dating as a way they can be together, and rightfully so. It's how God created us. But when there are no other outlets for knowing and being known, it's no wonder that sexual relationships are on the rise.

Sexuality is the culmination of knowing. All the walls come down in a sexual relationship, and we enter a relationship void of the false walls created by society. You can't very well hide much of anything when you're engaged in a sexual relationship with someone. Sure, sexuality is meeting a physical need. But more importantly, it's a place where teenagers are searching for true companionship.

Unfortunately, our culture rarely allows for teens to reach out and know each other honestly. Every second of their lives is plagued with a sense of making sure they fit in. If anyone steps out to be different, they're often made fun of or ostracized. If they think they've found someone who loves them for them . . . well, there you have it.

We can start mending the desire if we take a longer look at what God's intentions for relationships really are. If we can help students understand how to be in friendships that have core values of honesty, respect, and honor, they can have the emotional intimacy they long for with friends—without the physical intimacy boyfriends and girl-friends share. The beauty of having a relationship void of sexuality is that you get all the emotional and spiritual connection without the baggage of sex.

Too many kids are deceived by the misconception that sexuality is the only way to truly be in a companion relationship. That's why youth groups, summer camps, small groups, and sports teams need to strive to facilitate real relationships among teens. It's not as easy as saying, "Don't have sex 'cause God says so." We've got to get to the heart of the need—companionship—and provide a healthy alternative.

Reason #2: To Know How to Treat Each Other

I deal with teenagers all the time. They are the most selfish, inconsiderate, thinking-only-about-what's-beneficial-for-them demographic in our culture—and I *love* them.

The idea that a boy should open doors for a girl has gone by the wayside.

The notion that a text message can take the place of a conversation isn't considered odd.

And paying for a meal . . . Well, I've seen more guys than ever before expect girls to pick up the tab for dinner.

What happened to the days when guys knew how to treat a girl? When our actions really mattered and we told someone how much we valued them as a person?

When I was in college, a neo-movement began in the Christian community called courtship. Courtship is an almost ceremonial set of rules that a boy must follow in order to prove himself worthy to a girl's parents in order to date her.

In courtship . . .

The guy has to ask the dad out first.

The couple only goes on certain dates within certain times, to certain places, with certain people.

They set boundaries for their physical relationship.

And, ultimately, courtship is supposed to lead to a marriage vow.

In this model, there is no such thing as casual dating. When a boy shows an interest in a girl, there's an understood reason for his interest: mainly marriage.

But what if, in the middle of courting, you find out that you don't want to marry each other?

Isn't that the purpose of dating?

Some dates are going to be good.

Others are not going to be so good.

Some people are going to have chemistry.

Others are not.

Some are going to need boundaries.

But others are going to have freedom due to location or circumstance.

To make a sweeping declaration of courtship is to set couples up for long-lasting dead relationships. There's no spontaneity.

No sense of adventure.

There's no making decisions on the fly.

And many find courtship to feel more like a prison than a romantic discovery.

(Please hear me on this: I certainly believe there is a time to properly court a woman, but dating in high school or college isn't necessarily it.)

Courtship can be a useful tool to teach a man and a woman how to treat each other, and certainly there are a lot of practices inside courtship that I totally agree with, but my generation took it way too far.

Why can't we teach kids what it means to *care* for one another?

We can still help guys understand that how they look when they pick up a girl matters.

We can still help teens understand the importance of setting boundaries.

And while we're at it, we can still remind them (and ourselves) that parents are an important piece of this dating puzzle.

Let me propose this: Instead of applying another strict set of rules and regulations to a coed relationship, let's spend some time worrying about the reasons *why* we date and allow that to guide our motives and discussions. With a heartfelt understanding of why a gentleman should open the door, pull out a chair, take some initiative, and respect the rules set by Mom and Dad, we may see dating practices turn back in that direction.

We can do this! Teens want it. Teens need it. They want some boundaries in their dating lives, and they need to know how to put them into practice.

We can't sit back and just expect gentlemen to emerge from a culture that focuses on soliciting and glamorizing the sexual needs of people. We've got to share the truth and beauty of God-ordained sexual relationships and let teens know how this differs from what they see on TV. Moms and Dads, this starts at home.

Moms, help your boys understand the value of respecting a lady. Help them by demanding that they treat you like a lady. I see so many teenage boys running all over their parents, and parents just roll their eyes, as if to say, "Well, I can't do anything about it."

Yes, you can.

You're the parent.

You've got the keys to the city.

You've got the keys to the car.

You're providing the roof they live under.

You're providing the food they eat.

There are plenty of ways you can help your boys understand how to respect women, and adults in general.

Dads, you can help too. Help your boys understand what a wonderful impression they can make on a girl when they treat her right. Show them how much you respect your wife: Take time to notice her and say nice things to her in front of your kids. Show them how much you value the relationships you have, and those values will be passed on by observation.

You might think they're not looking, but every move you make is an impression you're leaving on the future of your son or daughter.

It's about being kind to one another.

But just because we are modeling manners at home doesn't mean we can automatically turn it all over to our teenagers and expect them to merely learn by observation. Modeling is only one element of teaching positive, healthy behavior. Dating is a learned behavior, and we've got to engage.

Moms, date your sons.

Dads, date your daughters.

I'm not being creepy here. I promise.

Moms, expect and accept nothing less than gentlemanlike behavior from your sons while modeling the behavior of a lady. Engage in meaningful conversation. ("How was school?" "Fine." does not apply.) Listen to his ideas, and teach him to listen and respond thoughtfully to yours.

Dads, treat your daughters like respected ladies. Tell them they're beautiful and honored. Then they'll accept nothing less from pursuing boys. Talk about the practical things you do as a way to help them learn. And then you've at least set them up for success when the time comes to start dating. We have to start teaching teenagers how to deal with one another on a one-on-one basis.

Are they going to make mistakes? YES!

Are they going to have skeletons in their closets? YES!

Are they going to regret some things in life? YES!

But that's what builds a person's character.

No one ever said dating was going to be easy.

No one ever said marriage was going to be easy.

Every relationship we have in life helps shape and mold our character into the people we are. To deny teenagers that same education is asking for a sterile world with no problems—and that's just not the world we live in.

I recently had a parent e-mail me and ask, "How can I be sure my kids stay on the right path as they go through high school?"

I thought for a while and then decided I didn't know how to answer.

The question was a bit presumptuous.

Somewhere in the hearts and minds of parents is a utopia where they can offer their kids something void of pain and hurt. Unfortunately, in the hearts and minds of parents is the only place this utopia exists. Of course, parents don't want their kids to go through hard times. Nobody wants to comfort a daughter when a boy breaks up with her. Nobody wants their boy to struggle with sexual thoughts or mistakes made in a relationship, but isn't that what real life is?

There's no such thing as a perfect dating relationship.

There's no such thing as a perfect marriage.

For that matter, there's no such thing as a perfect life.

We're all on a long journey to figure out how to make right decisions, and we'll all be guilty of making wrong ones. That's what makes us who we are.

I remember sitting in my father-in-law's office one day, frustrated with how some of my relationships were going. It was just one of those days. I was venting a bit about how someone had hurt me, and I was trying to figure out how to deal with it.

He reached inside his desk and pulled out a picture of an old cowboy boot with a "Jesus Saves" spur on the side.

The boot was all beat up, and it obviously had been used.

He asked, "If you were going to wear a pair of boots, would you pick these or go buy new ones?"

"Ummm, well, obviously I would go get some new ones." (I hate smelly shoes.)

"No, you wouldn't. The beauty of these boots is the comfort, the fit, and the feel. These boots have been through the muck and mire of a cowboy life, but they're probably the most comfortable shoes in the world."

And then it all made sense. He was right.

Life isn't meant to be sterile.

The people we are today is a culmination of mountaintop experiences as well as the valleys that tend to fill us with character. We don't want to be sterile clean shoes. We want the highs and lows of life to make us into people of character.

I write all this not to wish you or your teenager harm in life experiences but rather to provide a different perspective when looking at how dating affects us. It's worth the trial and error to figure out how to work through dating relationships. We'll be people of valuable character as we allow God to guide us, mold us, and shape us.

I was recently talking with a little old gray-haired lady in L.A. She heads up a wonderful ministry to the poor in downtown L.A., and we had a couple of hours to share our views on the state of the union of teenagers today. In the middle of our fascinating discussion she said, "Andy, you know why teenagers suffer so much as adults, don't you?"

"No, ma'am. What do you think?"

"Parents have made growing up something of a painless experience."

"I'm sorry? I lost you there," I said with a bit of trepidation.

"When we grew up, we had to raise our food. We had to milk

the cows. We had the work on the farm for our livelihood. Today, teenagers want for nothing. They've got all the toys in the world, their grades are dictated by how much a mother or father bugs the teachers, and their friendships are merely a culmination of arm's length online social networking."

As I started thinking about what this wise woman was proposing, I wondered, *Have we set up a world where teenagers aren't allowed to feel the pain of a failed relationship? Have we created a world where the pain needed to grow has been eliminated by a stronger desire to make sure our kids won't ever feel it?*

I wonder if that may be the problem with the current model of dating in the Christian world.

The nineties brought a wave of Christian dating where couples wanted to avoid breakups at all costs.

But maybe, learning how to deal with the pain of letting someone down, or working through the issues of a dating relationship, might make our marriages even stronger in the future. I know it has mine.

Don't try to use the slippery slope argument on me here. I'm not advocating that we just throw teenagers into a pool of dating relationships and watch as they either sink or swim. We can train teens to develop valuable behaviors toward one another that can curb some of the hurt. And when they do make a mistake, we can help them be more reflective, learning from the mistake and correcting the behavior that caused it. Either way, we've got to start letting the rope out a little. Otherwise when they head out on their own, they're going to go wild.

According to the *Journal of Sexual Medicine*, 63 percent of teenagers are sexually active before they leave high school; 87 percent are active before they leave college.[2] This behavior will have a lifelong impact on their relationships. We can no longer ignore these statistics.

We can do this!

Let's lock arms and begin a movement to live life alongside our kids and help them develop deep, meaningful relationships.

Reason #3: To Know Who You Want to Marry

I've got to be honest: I didn't even think of marriage until I was on the verge of my rehearsal dinner. It never crossed my mind. It was always "that" time when I was going to grow up, but it was so far ahead of me that I really didn't pay any attention to it.

It's inconceivable, now that I look back on it. I mean, really? This was going to be one of the most important decisions of my life. Would I marry someone? Who? What would it be like? Where would we get married? How would it all go down?

Nope. I didn't think about it one time.

It wasn't deliberate. It wasn't like I was proactively trying to avoid the conversation. I just didn't think about it. Maybe it was the pressure of thinking I would have to care for someone. Maybe it was the fact that I thought once you got married, you had kids and then you died. I don't know why I didn't consider it, but I do know that I'm not alone.

One of my favorite sessions to teach is when I have all the boys and the girls together. I start helping them see the differences between boys and girls, how they think differently.

I tell the guys, "Now watch this."

"Okay, girls. I want anyone in this group to raise their hand if they have ever thought about their wedding day before."

About 99.99 percent of the girls' hands go up.

"How many of you have ever thought about your wedding dress?"

About 90 percent of girls' hands go up.

"How many of you have thought about your bridesmaid dresses?"

About 75 percent of the girls raise their hands.

"How many of you have thought about getting married indoors or outside?"

You get the point.

Then I turn to the fellas.

"Guys, how many of you have ever thought about what tuxedo you're going to wear on your wedding day?"

Usually one or two hands go up because teenagers always try to be a bit cheeky.

"How many of you have ever thought about your groomsman tuxedos?"

No hands.

"How many of you have ever thought about the flowers?"

No hands.

"How many of you have ever thought about your wedding night before?"

A generous roar usually accompanies that question because most boys dream of the day when they can start having "legal" sex.

And in that one brief interaction, a whole new world of discussion is opened.

My point is that you can't just throw a guy and a girl into a relationship without first helping them to see the differences in the ways they think. Marriage conferences all over the country have produced millions of dollars of product to help husbands and wives understand communication techniques.

What if we could help our teens use the same techniques?

While they're dating.

What if we could set them up to know if someone is worth marrying?

Before they marry them.

Girls are just different from boys. They talk about boys, shopping, school, jobs, education, music, movies, the latest styles, who said what at the party last night.

Most guys don't care about those things.

If it doesn't involve sports, blood, video games, or some sort of adventure, they just don't care.

I know this is grossly stereotypical, but the time I've spent with teens (and adult males) proves it's just a *fact* about most guys.

How are we supposed to help guys see the need to wait to have sex before they get married when every turn of culture is telling them the opposite?

How can we expect girls to wait for sexual relationships when we can't help them see how valuable they are without sex?

Marriage isn't on the hearts and minds of today's teenage boys. But what would happen if we introduced the value of marriage to our boys?

What if we helped girls understand their worth through the friendships they have?

What if we set the stage for a real marriage relationship?

I don't mean these fairy-tale dreams I hear at local youth gatherings.

I travel to churches and conferences all over the world.

I hear the latest "sex talks" created by the best youth speakers around the country.

And to be honest, I haven't heard an honest one yet.

I haven't heard anyone address how fun sex is. They talk about pleasure, but they don't talk about discovering sexuality with someone who doesn't know anything about it. They don't talk about the awkwardness of going from the "no sex" Christian culture to an "okay, now have it" relationship after the marriage ceremony. No one talks about how hard marriage is until you get married.

We need to set a realistic stage for our kids to see the beauty of marriage.

Marriage is the ultimate sharing of life.

There are good times.

There are hard times.

There are scary times.

There are times of immense joy.

There are times of sorrow and pain.

But marriage is what it is.

If dating is supposed to be a precursor to marriage, maybe it's time we give kids a realistic picture. In fact, I think this unrealistic picture plays more into the failure of long-term relationships than we realize.

A lot of Christians get married just so they can start having "legal" sex. We've put such a stigma on purity that we've forced our young people to "burn with desire" without helping them understand the fundamentals of intimacy. So, what if we could channel some of our energy in the dating talks toward a way to model healthy, pure dating? Do you think we can start a movement?

I think we can, or at least put a dent in the pain caused by dysfunctional dating relationships.

We can start helping kids avoid unnecessary sexual confusion.

We can help start marriages that will last a lifetime, rather than just a few years — or months.

And who knows?

With a little mentorship, we might just see a generation of healthy kids grow up loving God, and loving their mate just the same.

Dating is an exercise meant to help a guy or a girl understand who they are compatible with.

It's a wonderful adventure to help them understand boys were made to like girls, and girls were made to like boys.

I often wonder if some of the gender issues we are dealing with at younger and younger ages are all a result of a culture that has vilified dating and forced boys to just hang with boys and girls with girls.

What if we could walk through healthy platonic relationships celebrated by God's wonderful timing, void of the stuff that causes lifelong scars but full of the stuff that helps students grow into the design God made them for?

I believe in marriage.

I believe God has ordained men and women to celebrate

monogamous relationships here on earth.

I believe in the celebration that two people can experience as life deals them victory or tragedy.

But maybe kids can just date for a while, without all that pressure.

CHAPTER 2

WHAT TO LOOK FOR

I LOVE GOING to malls, school functions, or even college campuses to watch how guys and girls find each other. The game is such an obvious behavioral motivator. I mean, really, if you see a few guys hanging out at the mall looking over the balcony, what do you think they're doing? I can assure you they're not shopping.

Or you can watch some girls hanging out together, walking from store to store, and they probably *are* shopping. But when they see a handsome guy walk down the hallway, heads turn, and all of a sudden the game is on.

I have to go out on a limb here and say I don't know exactly what girls are thinking. I had to spend some real time in research. For starters, I asked twenty women what girls are really thinking when they're looking for a date. Even though I didn't understand many of the answers, I got some interesting data from the girls interviewed.

But when it comes to guys . . . well, I *am* one, so I know how most of them think.

Ladies, let me be frank with you.

Most guys travel in groups of twos or threes. They're like a wolf pack in hunt of prey. Two wingmen so you don't make a fool of yourself is an essential practice. And, in the case you might strike up a conversation with a girl, the others are instructed to simply fade into the background. If it gets a little strange, they can always pop in and help navigate you out of a sticky situation.

I think it's important for girls to understand how guys travel. It's really quite amusing as you watch things play out in real time.

In any event, when guys go on the lookout, their eyes are scouring the terrain. They really have nothing going on between the ears; they're just looking to see something beautiful.

(This reminds me: Parents and leaders, we need to help ladies understand that unless they want a guy who dates them *because* they have curves—*help a guy out!*—wear some clothes. When guys are out hunting, girls understand that the more scantily clad they are, the more his head is going to turn. It's not that he cares for her, finds her interesting, or has any interest in anything but her curves. We need to say clearly, "Please don't think that this automatic glancing gesture has anything to do with how he's going to treat you in the future." This is a common mistake many girls make: They dress for attention, but they don't take into consideration what kind of reaction they're going to get with that attention. We need to warn young women and remind them of the guy who's *still* going to like them when their curves go away. So spend some time helping teen girls understand what it means to *dress carefully*.)

Every time I teach teenagers about relationships, I always set up a place where they can tell each other exactly what they're looking for when they date. It's kind of fun, and teens love it. Let's be honest: Most teen boys are interested in food, sports, video games, and computers. Most teenage girls are interested in fashion, friends, school, sports, gatherings, and who has the latest "thing." But both guys and girls are interested in talking about dating. Boys will always be interested in talking about girls, and girls will forever be interested in talking about boys. Count on it.

I figure that if guys are honest and girls take notes, then maybe we can find those divine matches right in our audience. I mean, what better place to find someone to date than in a captured audience interested in reformatting the way we think of dating and sexuality?

As I mentioned before, my wife and I run a camp for teens in Colorado. Most of the kids who come are already interested in asking hard questions about how to relate their faith to real life. We try to make the most of those moments.

You can too.

Take some time.

Put together a forum of discussion.

Don't try to own the answers.

Let the teens come up with answers they can be most honest with.

It's important that they have the freedom to tell each other what dating means and that those facilitating the conversation don't try to steer it too much. I've seen youth leaders and parents try so hard to guide discussions toward their own agenda. Teenagers can smell that agenda within seconds. Don't try to tell them how to date just yet. Let them take a second and come up with their own answers.

Don't worry: Guys will be completely honest. They'll tell you they want a date who will pay for the date, cook them food, and do their laundry. They'll make jokes and laugh about it at first, but give it time. When it sinks in that you're just trying to show them what they are saying, it's a powerful moment.

Likewise, if girls will be honest, and the fellas will take notes, then they'll stop acting like knuckleheads and really focus on things girls want in a date.

Well, that's the goal anyway . . .

So take some time.

Get your group of students together.

Get a whiteboard, a chalkboard, or if you're in a church where you have access to technology, just open a Word document and start typing their answers. They need to see what they say up on a screen or a board. Don't let the conversation run aimlessly or you'll end up focusing on one particular example. The point of this exercise is to show teens what they think they want, how immature they really are, and to get them to think about who they *really* want to date.

Even if you walk away and think they've joked through the whole session, believe me: They're listening.

TWO DIFFERENT PERSPECTIVES

In a session, I usually start with the guys. I feel like they're tough enough to be grilled first, and usually the fellas get a lot of laughs. I want the girls to understand that guys think very differently than they do.

When a young man goes out looking for a date and sees an attractive young lady, there are ten thoughts that go through his mind:

1. Hot!
2. Wow, she's really hot!
3. Man, that could be the hottest girl I've ever seen. (See any trends here?)
4. I wonder if she has a friend for you. (to the wingman)
5. Look at those legs.
6. Wow, HOT!
7. We should go and walk closer.
8. Man, she's hot!
9. If hotness were a quantifiable number, she's a 100!
10. Dude, I'm the *bomb!*

See any consistent thoughts?

I realize this is a stereotypical way to think of men, but isn't it true? I've been working with teens for ten years, all over the world, and the answers are the same. Plus, remember, I *am* a guy. I can almost predict what the guys are going to say before they say it.

Men are visual creatures. It's the reason magazines ads that sell cars often feature women dressed in bikinis.

It's how AXE is a company selling deodorant, but the commercials are all about hot girls following the guys around because they smell good.

It's why *Sports Illustrated* spends millions of dollars on an annual swimsuit issue. *Sports Illustrated* isn't trying to sell bikinis; it sells sports news. But who reads about sports? Who do you think the target audience is? *Men!*

It's not rocket science.

It's not a surprise.

Ever since the caveman days, men have looked at women and seen them as something to conquer.

It's just the way it is.

We don't have to deny it.

We just need to start understanding how boys think, why they think that way, and how girls might be able to navigate a relationship, knowing the facts.

I tell the guys, "Don't be ashamed of liking to look at women. That's how God made you." I remember sitting in a dating seminar once where the youth leader was trying to convince the group that attraction isn't important. I sat with my mouth wide open. "Are you kidding me?" Attraction is so important.

We don't need to teach guys to be ashamed for being the way God created them. As the theory of aesthetics plays into dating, "Beauty is in the eye of the beholder." And there are plenty of women who are beautiful to plenty of men.

The problem comes when beauty is regulated to a certain body shape, a certain height, or a certain weight. When the image of a woman is reduced to the illicit exploitation of a group of people, we get into trouble.

It's not a concern that guys want to date a girl who is good-looking. We just need to make sure we understand that "good-looking" is defined by how God made her.

Then I move on to the ladies and attempt to explain to the guys what girls are thinking.

"Fellas, when the ladies are out and about looking for a guy to call her own, she thinks . . ." And I leave this up to the girls. After all, they're the experts. "Ladies, give me a few phrases you think to yourself when a guy you're interested in walks down the hallway."

The list usually goes something like this:

1. Hot! (understandable)
2. Is he tall enough if I wear heels? (a little laughter)
3. Look at his eyes . . . and his teeth. (a little more laughter)
4. Does his last name match my first name? (an uproar)
5. What kind of job is he going to have?
6. What kind of car does he drive?
7. Is he creative when he asks me out?
8. Will he care for me?

You can see quite clearly that the lists are pretty different.

The ladies have a very comprehensive view of the opposite sex, while the guys are pretty much focused on their own visual satisfaction.

I spend a fair amount of time trying to process this notion.

How is it that guys are so interested in outward appearance, and women seem to have a little more depth? Surely it's not because guys are just animals. That's the very reason I'm writing this book. I don't believe we are just animals giving in to natural carnal lust. If that's the case, then we should nix dating and get it off the table of options.

But if we can begin to help teenage boys see the difference in girls . . .

And if we can begin helping teenage girls understand how boys think . . .

I truly believe we can begin a process of education that will lead us to healthy dating.

Now, with that being said and the groundwork being laid, I can start asking some of the real questions that I love watching teens answer.

"Fellas, what do you look for in a date?"

The list begins:

1. Hot! (of course)
2. A good cook (usually by some jokester in the audience)

They go on with these crazy answers—I let it go for a while—until they realize I'm trying to get to the heart of the issue. *Then it gets real!*

1. Sincere
2. Loving
3. Compassionate
4. Able to have a conversation
5. Sense of humor
6. Someone who has fun
7. Low maintenance
8. Someone who eats
9. Someone who likes sports
10. Someone who likes to hunt
11. She has friends
12. She has her own life
13. We can talk about anything
14. She likes spending time with me

Isn't it interesting?

When you get down to it, some of the stuff guys need in a relationship are the same things girls need.

They're not just animals.

They're not machines.

Boys have feelings.

They have needs.

They want similar things to what girls want.

But our society has created this "tough guy" image so guys can't reveal it.

They have to mask the insecurities of manhood with some sort of caveman, egotistical image in order to be thought of as a real man. (But that's the next book, *How to Be a Man in Today's Teenage Culture.*)

I truly believe that even though guys try to hide behind their visually oriented makeup, God created both men and women for companionship. That's why guys and girls enjoy being together. It's not simply because of hormones and puberty. God made us to get along.

He created us to enjoy one another's company.

He told Adam in the garden, "It is not good for the man to be alone" (Genesis 2:18). And He made Eve. That's the way the system works.

My hope is that guys will accept the way God created them and know that it's okay to like being with a girl, that it's okay to be friends with a girl and not feel like you have to be committed to marry someone or commit your life to someone, and because of that they can befriend a girl and it will be sincere.

They can feel good about a girl who knows the way they think.

They can feel secure about a girl they can sit and eat a meal with, without trying to perform this made-up "I have to figure out how to kiss her in order to be a man" syndrome.

That's how I met my wife.

I didn't have the most exemplifying dating record, but when I met Jamie Jo, everything changed. I didn't have any idea there was a woman in the world who would care for my heart the way Jamie Jo would.

It all started on a Monday morning in Old Testament class . . .

We were both attending Baylor University in Waco, Texas, a school that used to require you to take an Old Testament class and a New Testament class for your undergraduate work. Baylor also had a rule that you had to attend 70 percent of your classes or the professor had an obligation to fail you. (That's right; students *had* to go to class!) At the beginning of the class, everyone was sitting in various seats. But then the professor decided to create a seating chart to make recording attendance easier in his classes.

For whatever reason, I showed up early one day and sat in the front row. It happened to be the day our professor was making the seating chart, so from that day forward I was going to sit right there in the front row.

About three minutes before class started, this girl stumbled into class and looked at me sitting in the front row. She huffed in disgust, glared at me, and took her place right behind me in the only open seat in the class. Evidently she had been sitting in that very seat in the previous classes, and she felt like I had stolen her seat.

"I'll go find somewhere else," I said, noticing she was annoyed.

"No, I'll sit right here behind you," she said.

And that was the beginning.

For the next three or four months, Jamie Jo and I became best friends. We talked about everything.

We studied late at Denny's.

We started having lunch together.

She came to my intramural games.

I went to hers.

I was dating another girl at the time, and Jamie Jo would help me work through what a girl might be thinking in certain dating situations.

I was so insecure about dating. I didn't know how girls thought. And Jamie Jo offered me a sense of confidence.

She didn't care how I dressed.

She didn't care who I hung out with.

She was interested in getting to know me for me.

I was hanging with the guys and trying to figure out the fraternity world, and she helped me figure out which group of guys to hang with.

I was working through my future career, and she helped me think about what I was good at and what really made me love life.

We spent lots of time together, and it was great.

Even as I write this story and take a long, romantic walk down memory lane, I can still feel those same feelings of longing. It wasn't an erotic feeling at first. Neither of us wanted to seal the deal in marriage on our first meeting. But there was something special about how we related to one another.

It was like . . . I couldn't live without her.

Parents and youth leaders, hear this loud and clear: We must *teach* our kids a countercultural understanding of how we relate to one another.

Maybe start with these:

- Gentlemen, we need to recognize girls aren't objects to conquer.
- Ladies, there are guys out there who need your counsel.
- Gentlemen, ladies want to be treated with respect and dignity.
- Ladies, guys need a woman who will be loyal and trustworthy.
- Gentlemen, friendship is at the heart of knowing a woman.
- Ladies, friendship is at the heart of knowing a man.

FRIENDS WITHOUT BENEFITS

I believe dating is possible if we can eliminate the anxiety of trying to prove something sexually in a simple friendship. Guys need to be okay with getting to know a girl for who she is and not for what she can give him. Girls need to feel like they can relax and be themselves around guys, without all of the sexual pressure.

On the other end of the spectrum, under some Christian standards, people think if a girl goes on a date with a guy, she's forever bound to him. And to be fair, there are some guys who feel if they take a girl out for dinner, they have to be exclusive. No wonder kids are under such pressure. Can you imagine being sixteen and feeling like you have to be committed to someone for the rest of your life?

Just walk the hallways of today's high schools and watch how teens deal with the pressure from both sides. Couples either wear one another's clothes, share lockers, have all their classes together, and spend every waking moment trying to be together *or* they let the pendulum swing to the other side, and they don't have any sort of connection to commitment.

I was talking to a guy who goes to a pretty big high school in Dallas, Texas, and he was articulating the mood at his school.

"Andy, it's crazy. My friends will go out together, and somewhere during the night they all start pairing up. It usually leads to guys and girls making out all night, and then the next day at school it's like nothing ever happened. It's truly *friends with benefits*."

Even though he is steeped in this culture, he *knows* this isn't the way it is supposed to be.

But does he — how do *we* — change the norm?

I apologize if it feels like I keep hitting the same gong, but if hooking up is the sum culmination of dating, then I'm not for it. I don't think a healthy relationship can be a chance physical encounter without any sort of care or concern. And there's a distinct correlation between the damage it's doing to the psyche of our teenagers and how they view marriage.

No wonder affairs are so common.

No wonder online relationships are popping up all over the place.

No wonder guys are running off with the first woman who meets a new need.

THEY'VE BEEN TRAINED.

Commitment doesn't matter.

Feelings for someone can't go beyond the moment.

There's no consequence for hooking up.

It's just how we live life today.

Dating cannot be something we simply use for a license to make out. It has to be more, or we need to throw in the towel and call this practice of dating out of touch with reality.

In the last ten to fifteen years, many religious groups have reduced their opinion of teenagers to sexual misfits. They don't want sex education taught or condoms handed out at school on the basis of too much sexuality, but they've taken it to the extreme. I've watched as the uncomfortable nature of teaching sex turns into a full-blown "stick your head in the sand" mentality. There are those who think if we don't teach them, they won't know.

COME ON!

As Martin Short told Steve Martin in *Father of the Bride*, "Welcome to the nineties, Mr. Banks." You can't expect your teenagers to exist in the world and remain totally ignorant of the sexual tension in our culture. Even the most innocent movies on the silver screen contain a hint of boys who like girls. Just look at the latest Disney movie, and you'll see a princess and a prince who are trying to get together in the end.

When those seeds are planted and then watered with the ads during this week's sporting event: *Eureka!* You have a mind that is primed and ready for figuring out sexuality. So let's be careful how we look at sex education in our world today. Sure, we don't want people training our kids in sexual behavior that is deviant, but *someone* has to step up to the plate and help them rethink sexuality in our world. If it's not parents or youth leaders, then just get ready: Lady Gaga, Lindsay Lohan, Justin Timberlake, and whichever latest celebrity they look up to will teach them.

It's almost as if the broad Christian community has given in to the worldview that says teenagers can't date without having sex; therefore, we need to outlaw dating. May it not be so. We need to help educate teens how to date *correctly*. We need to teach them to learn about each other, to test the dynamics in a male/female relationship, to have fun together, to work out disagreements together, to care for one another as human beings, as girls and guys.

Every day, all day long, the world is teaching teens that relationships are only physical.

We must be louder than the world.

We must teach them that relationships are social, emotional, biblical, educational, meaningful, wonderful experiences.

Parents and leaders, we can teach our teenagers how to do this. It just takes some intentional time. It takes some vulnerability. It takes some real willpower to allow our teens to grow up and begin thinking about what it might look like for them to enter into a relationship.

We want this to happen.

We need this to happen.

We celebrate it when it goes well.

Can you imagine someone with no education in engineering building a bridge over a body of water in your local town? Imagine a town that said, "Well, we just don't want kids to think too much about these wild ideas of math and science." So when it was time to build a road to get over to the other side, an innocent person who'd been watching *How It's Made* on the Science Channel volunteered to build it.

Would you drive across that bridge?

Do you think in your wildest imagination that bridge would stand the test of time, weather, and traffic?

Of course not.

So why should dating be such a taboo when it comes to teens?

Parents, they can do it. I believe in them.

Will they make mistakes? Sure.

But unless we're willing to help educate them to date well . . .

Unless we're willing to walk with them through the mistakes . . .

Unless we have a goal of successful marriages in mind . . .

THEY WILL FAIL!

I *believe* teenagers can do it.

They're not mindless animals that can't control themselves, as my Darwinist friends would claim.

With a little training, a little modeling, and a lot less pressure, teenagers can start being friends with a boy or a girl and discover the nuances of the opposite sex.

Unfortunately, our culture injects so much pressure for kids to "prove" their love to one another; it's almost impossible to stand up for something you believe in so strongly without being weird, strange, or totally out.

My son Hays is in fifth grade. He came home a few weeks ago and told me some kids were "going together," and the other kids on the playground wanted them to prove their relationship. They put the two kids in a closet and told them they had to French kiss so everyone would know their true devotion to one another.

My first reaction? I laughed out loud. Then after I composed myself, I looked at him and said, "What?"

Hays said the little boy came out of the closet (no pun intended there) crying his eyes out. The girl was so embarrassed that she skipped the rest of recess and went straight back in to her class.

What kind of culture do we live in?

Why are ten-year-olds trying to prove their love to one another?

Is the media teaching our kids about dating?

Is it moms and dads who are engaged in the dating world after divorce?

Is it older brothers and sisters who are sharing these principles with younger kids?

Who knows where it's all coming from? There's probably some truth in saying the pressure is a combination of all of these things. But the facts are clear: Unless we start talking about dating and sexuality with our kids at a younger and younger age, we're leaving them to navigate these turgid waters on their own.

Let's be honest with ourselves: Boys were made for girls, girls were made for boys, and it's time we help the two understand the vast impact they can have on each other — before it's too late.

CHAPTER 3

SHOULD YOU HAVE A RELATIONSHIP?

WHEN WE LOOK at the question at hand—"Should teens date?"—it not only merits a "why" answer, but it also deserves a "how" answer.

Parents ask me all the time, "How old should my teenager be before I start letting him/her go out on dates?"

What a loaded question!

Sometimes parents are kind enough to share what their moral compass has demanded of them, but often it's an open-ended question, and people really want to know the answer.

With teenagers, I'm *really* clear.

If you're "going together" in the first grade, well, that's kind of silly. It's like playing house in the backyard in the tree fort—only you've committed the cardinal sin of every boyhood neighborhood hangout: *You invited a girl.*

It just seems kind of play-like.

The hardest answers come with the thirteen- to fifteen-year-olds. There's such a desire to grow up and be a part of society, and this age group often pushes parents to let them date before they are really ready to engage in any kind of relationship with the opposite sex. I mean, think about it . . .

If a teenager is thirteen, is he going to pick up his date on a skateboard to take her to the movies?

And if they somehow think having parents drive them to the mall makes it cool, don't be deceived. All the older kids are laughing at them when they jump out of Mom's car.

How are they going to pay for a date at thirteen? Ask Mom for the cash?

How can they have any idea how to care for someone else's well-being?

If you really want a definitive answer for when *I think* teens should even be thinking about any kind of alone dating, there's no biblical basis for it, but sixteen would be my minimum.

Still, I've found the maturity of most teenagers between age fifteen and sixteen makes them overwhelmingly *not ready to date*. But I am a dating proponent.

I believe in dating. (At least until my daughter reaches fifteen—then I'm writing another book titled *Don't Date till You're 40!*)

Really, the beauty of having teenagers beginning to explore relationships while they are at home is a true advantage. It was more than ten years ago when the book *I Kissed Dating Goodbye* first came out, and the dating world came unglued, especially in the Christian community.

Christians swallowed Josh Harris's argument for the abolishment of dating in our civilization, and even though Josh had a point, his premise was totally off.

What the book did was hurl a generation into a place where no one understood the simplest forms of relationship building. We became relational illiterates, a generation scared to talk to each other for fear they would have to commit to marriage.

(Josh, I know your heart and agree wholeheartedly that something needs to be done.)

Parents and leaders, we need to help our teens understand their God-given need for a relationship. It's *natural!* You can't just turn this on and off, and that's the ultimate problem. Boys were made for girls, and girls were made for boys. That's the way God intended it.

So what do we do?

I think it's helpful to look back at our own histories and see if we can come up with some solutions together.

THE CHRISTIAN COMMUNITY SAYS . . .
1. Don't have sex till you get married.

And then, all of a sudden, when our kids get married, we think they are guaranteed to have super-healthy sexual relationships. I can tell you from firsthand experience: It took a while to move past the threat of eternal damnation into having a vibrant sexual life.

For twenty-one years I was told sex outside of marriage was a bad thing. Then I put on a wedding ring at the front of some church, and my whole paradigm was supposed to just vanish and I was supposed to experience the joy of sexuality that God saved for marriage. I gotta tell you, it was very difficult.

And now, I counsel young married men *all the time* who are having issues with sexuality. Is it right? Is it wrong? How can I change what I think?

Can you imagine the mind game that must go on in a healthy sexually driven male or female when our community gives them the "get out of jail free" card at the altar?

They've gone to all the abstinence classes.

They've heard the sex talk every Valentine's Day.

Pastors continue harping about how sex outside of marriage is the cardinal sin in someone's life.

Then, all of a sudden, there was my wife lying in my bed, and I had to keep telling myself, *It's okay. Look at your left hand. You've got a ring on. It's all right.* I know that sounds weird, but if we're going to take this dating thing seriously, we have to identify all the problems. I used to think I was really weird, but when I started counseling more and more college students who were getting married, I found a common theme. People were getting married and waiting to engage in a sexual relationship for days or sometimes even weeks after the wedding night.

Now, don't read too much into that. I'm not proposing that we send our kids out to have sex now to temper their future marriages. What I am proposing is that we sit down and start talking *early and often*. We've got to start helping teens understand the pleasures of sex, the consequences of sex, and the design God made for sex in our lives.

Marriages with healthy sex lives need to be modeled. I'm not talking about making videos or going into the Christian porn industry, but how harmful would it be for a husband to teach a small group of guys, helping them to understand what sexuality is really like in marriage?

So many kids think sex is what they see in the movies or on TV. Boys have this image that sex is supposed to last for hours and hours until they have reached ultimate pleasure. How do you think they feel when they have their first experience and it's nothing like that?

They have a carnal attitude toward sexuality, and why not? It's exactly what they're being taught.

My wife talks to women *all the time* who are scared to death of their wedding night. Psychologically they're not prepared; physically they know only what they've seen in the movies or heard from their friends. Why is it such an awful thing to have a godly woman lead a group of teenage girls into a conversation about the reality of sex in marriage?

God made it.

He sanctioned it.

It's what makes us different, male and female.

Certainly we don't want to turn this section into some R-rated explicit conversation, but with care and couth, we can help our teens understand the reality of sexuality when they get married. We don't have to dismiss them from the conversation and fear they'll run out and try it with each other. Let's just open the conversation and help them have a real, grounded way of thinking about sexuality within the confines of a healthy marriage.

Maybe we can also help their future relationship by opening up about the successes and failures we've learned along the way. It's so rewarding to hear teenage boys say, "Thank you for being honest," when we talk this way. They long for it. They need it. They're looking for someone who can shoot them straight about the taboo topics of life.

Our kids are learning about sex from movies, pop stars, and magazines because *they're the only ones talking*. We need to join the conversation. We need to inject the truth.

2. Don't date unless you're ready to marry.

Are you kidding me? It's no wonder that kids out there are exploring in secret. We've created this authoritarian pseudo-necessity for kids to navigate alone, and then we hold them to it. We've created a culture where you have to have a serious interest in marrying someone before you even go out on a date. As the Joker asked in the 2008 movie *The Dark Knight*, "Why so serious?"

Fathers of girls are giving guys the fifth degree, thinking it is their God-given duty to keep the boys out. I totally understand. As a father, I get it. But, dads, we gotta give the guy a fighting chance, right? Think back to the time you went to pick up your first date. You didn't really appreciate Grandpa out there polishing his nine millimeter.

I mean, it makes for a great story around the campfire during our annual guys trip. Can you see it? A bunch of old guys sitting around joking and laughing, and then one pipes up with a great story of how he made the latest acne-infested boy run from his house in terror. There's something remarkably sadistic about it, but let's be honest: It's fun!

We have a state of being with our "dad friends" where we are the toughest show in town — and I gotta be truthful, there's good reason. Have you walked through the malls and movie theaters these days? Have you seen the guys we're entrusting our future to? Okay, I get it.

I remember after Jamie Jo and I started dating, I went up to meet the family. This in itself was a miracle, knowing the history of ministry her family is involved in. Needless to say, I was a little intimidated.

I showed up at Spike and Darnell's house wearing my normal cargo shorts, T-shirt, and hat worn backward. I didn't think anything of it, and I wasn't really trying to impress after such a long journey to the most remote part of southwest Missouri.

I got out of my car.

Knocked on the door.

Hoping to find Jamie Jo answering.

But to my surprise it was her eighty-year-old grandfather.

He took one look at me, and I knew I had done something wrong.

You have to understand that Spike White is a legend in southwest Missouri. He was one of the grandfathers of Branson, traveled all over the world speaking to teenagers about coming to camp, and inspired more than one man to be a "real man." This guy had it all: He was gentle to his wife, caring to his kids, and loving to a community. He was a hero.

So here I am, a cocky college freshman showing up to spend the weekend with my friend, his granddaughter Jamie Jo.

He looked at me and said, "Boy, you know what the bill of a hat is for, don't you?"

"Uhhh, to cover my nose from the sun, I guess?"

"You're a smart one, aren't you?"

"Uhhh, is Jamie Jo here?" I asked after an awkward silence.

"Boy, if the bill of your hat is to cover your nose, why are you wearing it backward? Unless your parents did a lot of drugs in the sixties, your nose is on the front of your face!" he exclaimed.

"Sir, I'm just looking for Jamie Jo. I didn't mean to—"

"Oh, it's okay." He smiled, knowing he got me. "Come on in here. We've been expecting you."

I know it was a just a joke, and I can take a joke. But imagine how many dads (and granddads) are out there just waiting to use their latest trick on the boy coming to date their daughter. I know how valuable daughters are. I get it. I'm probably going to use some of the same.

But some of us have taken our job of protection and made it into a job of intimidation. Let's just say this: If the local boys in school are so scared of you they won't talk to your daughter, good luck getting a quality son-in-law some day.

Why does it have to be like that?

There's a much better way to usher in a dating relationship. You can invite the guy in and tell him how valuable your girl is. You can begin a real-live friendship. You can show you daughter you are interested in the boys who come to pick her up. Dads, you can make this process part of developing community, rather than trying to shoot the next guy who comes to your house.

And moms . . . *oh my!*

Mothers are suspicious of every girl who walks through the front door. Moms, just because your son has a friend who's a girl doesn't mean she's going to steal your little boy away. It's natural. This is what's supposed to happen.

I believe there are two types of moms.

1. The Aggressor

This is the mom who looks for any indication of a female with her son. He starts talking of girls, and Mom sees the need to make sure there is no way they are ever going to break up. She invites the girl to every family outing. She orchestrates meetings with her son and girlfriend that will develop memories. She is working to make sure her son marries this girl. Aggressor moms, BACK OFF!

2. **The Protector**

The protector mom is a little different from the aggressor. She is the one who hawks over her son every chance she gets. She watches every girl who comes into contact with her son as if that girl is some kind of street worker trying to entice her baby boy into a harsh sexual relationship. Although protectors are needed in our culture, protector moms have to be careful. You can end up being the talk of the school as the crazy mom who doesn't trust anyone. And in the middle of all this, teenagers are *reeling*.

Girls are embarrassed and fearful that Dad is really going to bury a boy in the backyard.

Guys are scared to talk to a girl's parents.

Girls won't date at all just to keep the relationship with her parents at bay.

Guys won't talk to parents about dating for fear that they're going to be made fun of, their moms will marry them off, or their dads will embarrass them as they bring home someone special to introduce.

Whatever happened to good, old-fashioned friendship?

Can we allow a boy to invite a girl over and be friends? (If *not*, what message is *that* sending?)

What happened to a time when a girl and a boy walking through the halls of the local mall was considered an afternoon with friends rather than a sign that they're off to the chapel to get married?

Come on, folks. We need to settle this down a bit.

Dads, invite the young man into your house. Show him that you expect him to respect your family values, but there's no need to polish the gun.

Moms, spend some time with a young lady to see what kind of girl she really is. You can rest assured that how this young lady treats you is how she's going to treat your son, and it's important that you have an honest conversation with both kids about the relationships they're engaging in.

We don't need to hide in the corner and watch our sons and daughters try to figure it out on their own. We can help. Engage!

3. Parents need to respect their kid's privacy.

Christian or not, dating or not, the message that "Mom and Dad need to respect my privacy" is sent out by practically every teen that ever exisited.

But . . . *sorry!*

While kids are living under Mom and Dad's roof, they've got to understand and observe their rules. Parents, you have the right to respectfully engage in teen life as much or as little as you want. It's your God-given authority to make sure you're raising your kids. Teens think it's silly, but most parents have been through this dating thing before and have (hopefully) figured it out successfully.

Remind your teens that when it's time to listen, even when the ruling is hard, obedience is key. When God said, "Honor your father and your mother," it wasn't a suggestion (Exodus 20:12). If teens want to know the fullness of relationships through the eyes of the Lord, they've got to be teachable, coachable, and people who listen well.

E-mails are public forum.

Texts should be shared regularly.

Facebook friends need to be out in the open.

The more transparency teenagers give to their relationships, the better the chance of healthiness in their dating world.

I recently spoke with a mom who was angrily trying to figure out how to manage her son's communication with girls. "I just don't want to invade his privacy; he's got to have his space."

Excuse me? His space is limited to the phone you buy, the roof you pay for, and the food you give him for dinner. His space is your space.

Why should there be anything to hide?

If we are teaching our teens how to date in a godly way, then why would they want to hide anything from us anyway?

Believe me, I understand the need for teenagers to spread their wings and make decisions.

I've heard the argument: "Andy, he's sixteen, and in two years he's going to have to make his own decisions. I want him to learn how to make decisions under my roof."

But while they are under your roof, it's your call.

You decide the rules.

You decide the transparency.

You decide the policy.

If you have teenagers who are working to hide in private something they are scared to tell you in public, there's going to be something wrong.

And what a great way to teach communication. If you can help teenagers work through communicating the hard issues, you'll be setting them up for success that will last far beyond a high school dating relationship.

4. If I let my teenager date, I'm giving up.

Parents, let me give you the bottom line: If you want to have grand-children—*ever*—this is part of the process.

Either you can watch your kids start scheming in the dark shad-ows of high school, *or* you can help, guide, and direct them. You have a wonderful chance to become a part of the journey rather than a spectator. And the relationship you develop through the process will offer you a deeper understanding of your teenager.

"But what if my teen won't listen?"

Well, let me tell you what's going on in high school and college today. I think you'll find the next section of this book interesting. It's surprising and appalling, and if we're not ready to change course here, we're in for generations of relational failure.

I know this isn't easy.

But we can either let Britney Spears teach our kids how to handle relationships or start taking a proactive approach to *the* issue of the teenage world.

Whether or not we are ready to admit it, dating in some shape, form, or fashion is going to happen. And we can either talk about it, plan for it, and shape it *or* let it shape us into a culture void of and unable to experience real-time relationships with each other.

I'm a firm believer in the fact that, given the right circumstances, we can set teenagers up for a life of relational success rather than failure.

Will we . . .

Can we . . .

Do we have the guts to set a course for our teens and students so they might know the fullness of what God intended when He said that man shouldn't be alone?

CHAPTER 4

THE NEW DATING HORIZON

I SAT ACROSS the table from a group of fifteen-year-olds at a restaurant in a small U.S. town. Most of them were attending the private Christian school in the area, and most of them were old friends of mine.

I was enjoying the company, thoroughly enjoying the food, laughing, and catching up when all of a sudden the topic turned to dating.

"What did he say to her?"

"What did they do last night?"

"Where did you go?"

"What did you do?"

It was like sitting in a detective's office while he interrogates the criminals. But here, the answers were not only sought by the group, they were freely given by the individuals. I couldn't believe all the things they knew about their friends.

They were up to speed on just how far each one of them had gone physically.

They knew who would compromise their sexuality and who was going to save themselves.

They even knew which boys were the predators.

Out of nowhere I asked, "So how many students do you think are sexually active in your school?"

The conversation stopped. They looked at me like I was some alien from the planet Voltron and had just invaded their planet.

"Andy, you just don't get it, do you?"

"I guess not. What don't I get?" I asked innocently enough.

"Oral sex at our school is just not that big of a deal."

I was shocked. I couldn't believe my ears. Here was the high school popular crowd trying to convince me that oral sex was something considered more the norm than the exeption to the rule. What was going on?

I was determined to figure this one out.

What is really going on in the hallways of the public high school?

THE BIG SURPRISE

Later that year, I was speaking at a local youth event and had the chance to interview a group of twenty high school seniors. "Okay, tell me the real deal," I said. "What's going on in the hallways of your high school?"

I spent the next hour in utter shock as they revealed incidents of sex in the bathrooms, sex under the bleachers, sex at the dances, even the dreaded text hookup before the school-sponsored dance. It was *unbelievable!*

I had no idea.

There was no talk of flowers.

No creative ways that the boys were coming up with new dates.

No movies.

No dinners.

Just out-and-out raw sexuality.

High school parties are filled with teens interested in just hooking up.

They have a one-night physical relationship.

Then they walk the hallways the next day as if nothing ever happened.

As I sat there and listened, I wondered why.

How are so many high school students finding themselves in the middle of these torrid sexual relationships with no real way to understand how to communicate with one another?

"How many girls got pregnant this year at your school?" I asked.

And every one of them had stories of five to ten students in their school system who had to leave because they were pregnant.

Look, I believe in True Love Waits.

I think purity rallies are a good thing if we're raising awareness.

Purity rings work . . . sometimes.

But the fact of the matter is, all these programs we've come up with are still failing. They're failing miserably, and there's little to no hope that an entire generation is going to change without significant help.

It's not because the intentions of these programs aren't pure. They are. I've spoken to hundreds of True Love Waits crowds about dating, sexuality, and what it means to be in a meaningful relationship. It's not that we don't have the right information; the real problem centers around the way we deliver it.

There's no question that early active sexual relationships are harmful to our development.

There's no question that the chances of physical disease increase as teenagers sleep from bed to bed.

There's no question that the psychology of today's teenagers is severely hindered when they are actively engaged in sexual partnerships.

The problem lies in the ability teenagers have to compartmentalize every area of their lives.

I remember sitting with Chap Clark at a large teenage conference. He wrote a book called *Hurt*, which outlines issues teenagers deal with on a day-to-day basis. He talks about relationships with parents and friends, school pressures, and culture. But one of the most interesting parts of Dr. Clark's research is the comparison of the teenage brain.

It's no secret that teens have the ability to see themselves with different reputations depending on the crowd they are with. Just go look at their Facebook profiles. You'll see some kids who put "Christian" as their religious preference, but if you peruse their photo albums, you'll see a lifestyle that is anything from the life Jesus called us to live.

Businesses have figured this out, as some now require access to your Facebook profile as a contingency of employment. Employers want to know who they are hiring and what kind of advertisement an employee will be to the public.

This compartmentalizing doesn't change just because we're talking about dating.

Today's teenagers can go to a purity rally on Friday night at six o'clock and be in bed with their boyfriend or girlfriend by ten o'clock—and think nothing of it. The rules have changed. There's no connection between belief and commitment anymore, primarily because we have modeled an inconsistent Christian lifestyle.

One girl told me, "Andy, you don't get it. Oral sex is like holding hands at my school. It's just what you do."

And once again, my spirit dove into that dark place where hopelessness reigns.

What is going on?

It's hard to accept that someone might be able to live a Christian life on Sunday and Wednesday, and then live as though they've never graced the threshold of a Christian church for the rest of their lives.

But realistically, that's who we're dealing with.

Teenagers have a home life, a school life, a friend life, an entertainment life, an online life, and a dating life. There are so many different compartments in the mind of today's teenagers, and they have trouble keeping up with which one is which. This is another reason teenagers are struggling with relationships.

When the lights are out and the door is closed . . .

When there's nobody around . . .

When all they can think about is *Who am I?* and God is the only one in the room . . .

Teenagers are struggling to answer life's most basic question. They don't know if their movie life lines up with their home life. They don't know if their video game life is the same as their Christian life. They never intersect.

So you can see the major problem we have here.

If we teach abstinence at a conference or in a group, how can we expect the great compartmentalization experts to relate that teaching to their real life?

THE MEDIA MADE ME DO IT

Britney. Christina. Miley. Madonna. Lady Gaga. Pamela Anderson. Lindsay Lohan. Paris Hilton.

All women who are influential in the media.

All women who have expressed sexuality in different ways.

All women who are emulated as "sex symbols" in our culture.

I recently was interviewed with some of the top denominational leaders in the country. "Why do you think our next generation is leaving the church in record numbers?"

Without a doubt . . .

Without hesitation . . .

Without even a blink of their eyes . . .

"IT'S THE MEDIA!"

Okay, can we really think about this for a second?

There's no doubt you can see an onslaught of sexuality in the media today. The things shown in commercials during NFL games would make the hair on the back of my grandfather's neck stand up in offense. Times have changed.

More and more movies are including more and more explicit sexual contact at lesser and lesser ratings. PG-13 movies now have full frontal female nudity.

Television shows are breeching the boundaries of obscene as we watch more and more characters express their sexuality in real time on network TV.

We live in an "oversexed" culture. I will concede.

But I'm tired of hearing how the media made anyone do anything.

If you're shot, will you try to sue Smith & Wesson because they made the gun? It's the same logic.

A gun didn't shoot anyone.

Someone with a purpose picked up a tool and pulled a trigger. Guns don't shoot people; they are inanimate objects. It was an improper use of the gun that led to the shooting, so to place the blame on the gun is to merely remove the responsibility of the person who should have to learn gun safety.

The same is true with the media.

It's not the media's fault that we have a sexually immoral genera-tion. We're simply acting out and using the media in improper ways. To add insult to injury, if we didn't use the media the way we're using it today, then they wouldn't make the kinds of media they make today. It's simple supply and demand. If producers and directors are trying to make a profit off a particular medium, they're not going to create something that doesn't sell. And if we were a group of people intentional about salvaging the remaining moral compass in our culture, we wouldn't give them reason to make the kinds of media that are distorting our view of sexuality. You see, it's a vicious cycle.

So what do we do about the media's influence on our culture?

We spend time helping students walk through it — together.

Remember, rules without relationships produce rebellion. If

we're intentional about giving students a way to walk through the medium of television, movies, music, books, the Internet, or whatever media they're using today, we can help them think about the choices they make as they relate to real life.

Let me give you an example.

The largest-grossing movie released in 2009 was a film directed by the famed James Cameron. Mr. Cameron directed movies like the *The Terminator* in the eighties, *Titanic* in the nineties, and now *Avatar*.

Avatar is a film about an alien group of people living on a planet far, far away that is invaded by humans. The humans have discovered a resource that demands high dollar, but in order to mine the resource, they've been forced to develop relationships with the native people groups in an attempt to get them to relocate. The visuals of this science-fiction film are nothing short of awe-inspiring as the scientists use cloned bodies to literally represent them to the natives as they develop friendships, share educational techniques, and ultimately drill into their land.

Now, if you ask why more than $1 billion was spent in the United States alone to watch this movie, you'll get a wide variance of response.

I liked the visual effects.

I liked the story.

I liked the way it demonstrated colonization in a fictional way.

Whatever . . .

There are a couple of scenes in *Avatar* that speak directly to the nature of sexuality. The main character develops a relationship with one of the natives, and their love goes against the ancient traditional ways of her people to mate.

At first glance, someone might say, "Don't go see that movie *Avatar*. It represents sexual deviance in relationships."

Remember, rules without relationships lead to rebellion.

So many movies promote a lifestyle of free sexuality without consequence. The leading man takes the leading lady home, and it's all normal. There's no movie I know of that deals with the after-effects of sexuality. Well, maybe *Juno*.

In this popular movie, a teenage girl confesses her pregnancy to her parents, deals with kids at school, and ultimately tries to find life after an accidental pregnancy. *Juno* was a great look into the heart of a teenager, but in the end it was almost like the audience was meant to celebrate — rather than feel sorry for — the girl.

Great movie, by the way. I'm a huge *Juno* fan. It taught a lot of teenagers that it is okay to deal with pregnancy.

And that's what teenagers don't understand.

Life changes once a girl becomes pregnant.

If she decides to have an abortion, she lives with the very real guilt of killing another human.

If she decides to carry the child, she lives with the shame and embarrassment she feels around her family, friends, and often at church.

Most of the time, she thinks life is going to continue on like in the movies instead of understanding that now she has to take care of another human — and it changes *everything*.

So what if we took the medium being used by our culture — mainly movies — and began to teach our students how to proactively think about the ideas being presented and the consequences that would happen in real life?

What if we started asking questions about how sexuality was really being portrayed in the story and probed our students for real-life examples where it might not always wind up with a happy ending?

You see?

A major hurdle that has to be jumped before we can throw the TV out the window is to recognize the way our culture is using media to seed ideas into the hearts and minds of students. And instead of leaving these ideas alone to take root inside the minds of our teens, let's address them head-on.

We must trust the "greater is he that is in you, than he that is in the world" principle (1 John 4:4, KJV) to get past our obsession to create some evil empire that is luring our culture away from traditional values. As we help kids walk through the ideas, identifying the ways those ideas don't work in real life, we can stand confident that God's spirit will rule.

I know it's a hard shift to make. And I'm certainly not advocating that we open the gates and watch every single movie that is created. But, instead of crying out, "The media made me do it!" all the time, maybe we can take a logical approach and help students understand the whys of the medium.

Why doesn't sexuality work when expressed like it was in *Avatar*?

What were the undertones of the movie that led us to believe that the "truth" expressed by the film wasn't actually workable in real time? What would you do differently?

And it doesn't stop with movies.

Britney Spears has a song called "If You Seek Amy."

That title phrase, when sung, spells out a pretty bold message: F#$% me.

Kids know this.

And what's more indicative of our culture is that they laugh like they're getting away with something.

Moms and dads are passively sitting by, wondering why sexual behavior is happening, and our culture is pressuring kids to hide their own sexuality. Teens feel like they can live in the shadows of cute lyrics, when all the while their inner passion is awakened, encouraged, and sometimes called normal.

WAKE UP, PARENTS!

WAKE UP, YOUTH LEADERS!

Music affects your kids. They might try to lull you into thinking they only listen to the beat or the musical talent of a particular artist, but don't be fooled. Try it!

Go to www.billboard.com, a site that charts the most popular music of the day. If you look at the "Hot 100" list, you'll see the top one hundred songs playing in America that day. Believe me, you won't have to go too far to see the latest and greatest artist talking all things sexuality.

Often, I will play a Top 40 song for the kids I speak to and just sit and watch their reaction. Usually they stand up and dance to the song; it didn't get a Top 40 spot because Christian teenagers decided to turn the dial on the radio when the song came on. Actually, pop music hits the charts because our culture buys into the idea that either it's good music or it speaks to a particular philosophy of the day.

Teens know these songs. They'll recite them for you. And we wonder . . . why do they think about sexuality the way they do?

If you want to take it to the next level, put the lyrics on a screen and ask students to look for the message being sung by the artist. I can spend hours with kids dissecting the effect of pop culture on our worldview, and usually we come away with real truths.

Does it mean every kid will stop listening to a particular type of music?

No.

But when we expose the truth for what it is, when kids begin allowing the ideas planted in their hearts to grow, they have a method of processing those ideas in the light of a biblical worldview.

I don't advocate the destruction of Hollywood. I want to help students where they are. They're watching new releases, listening to new songs, and surfing the Internet for whatever reason. If we can give them tools to interpret, then we won't be innocent bystanders as images cross the television screen; we'll be proactive thinkers about the way life really works.

I'm amazed at the cognitive skills teenagers can use once they have the tools to do so. They know when something is right or wrong. The Bible says that it is "written on their hearts" (Romans 2:15). So when we enforce those laws and help them to reach a point of understanding, we stop allowing the media to dictate or shape our views on sexuality.

Imagine a world where teenagers would collectively be able to say, "Those two people in the movie may have hooked up, but I know that relationship won't continue on in happiness without some boundaries and attention to detail."

It can happen.

I've seen it happen.

And I believe if we're a little more careful in how we approach the media—instead of making the media the evil of our day—we can use the messages to teach valuable lessons.

I do think media plays a role, but it's not the sole reason kids are having sex. I think it goes much, much deeper than what music they're listening to or what movies they're watching. It's friends. It's environment. It's pressure. It's uneducated dating groups. It's a combination of a whole variety of worldviews knocking on the doors of their hearts.

There are several ways we can attack this problem, but we've got to be willing to stand up and think. We can't just tell kids to stop watching television or listening to the latest hip-hop music and think it's all going to go away. We're in much deeper than that.

THE BIGGEST ISSUE

Hooking up is a result of the central theme I keep running into, and sexuality is just one symptom of a larger problem.

Every human is designed and created to be with others. We've seen this in Genesis. But the tricky part of understanding this verse is recognizing that Adam wasn't alone in the garden.

He was walking with God.

He was talking with God.

He was enjoying the richest relationship any man has ever had with the Creator of the universe.

Yet God saw fit that he live life with other humans.

At every turn our culture tries to make us feel like we are so closely connected with one another, doesn't it? Just surf the net, look at the latest social networking site, and you can see the false impressions of togetherness we fall victim to every single day.

The greatest social-network experiment in the history of the Internet is Facebook. According to Facebook's stats, there are more than 500 million users worldwide. That's almost twice the population of the entire United States.[1] Five hundred million is an unbelievable number.

Facebook is set up to cater to the most intimate parts of the human condition. We all desire to be "with" others; it's ingrained in who we are as people. It's the exact reason God had to create other humans. We need each other to meet various needs and desires, but ultimately I believe we all have an intrinsic need to be together. Facebook provides a technological way to hit that need by its very infrastructure.

Every time there is a connection on Facebook, it's masked as being a "friend." To date, I have more than five thousand "friends," but the problem lies in the very nomenclature. The word *friend* has been used on Facebook to allow for photo transfers, wall posts, and even a private inbox function, all without hearing, seeing, or interacting personally with any of your "friends."

Facebook has provided a wonderful way for old friends to reconnect who might not have otherwise known contact information, but it's indicative of the way the new generation is forming relationships. If you can be "friends" behind the impersonal laptop screen, what good is there in sharing who you really are at the core of your being. Behind the computer screen, you can be anyone you want. You can say, "I'm fine," and even though you might be struggling through a hard time in life, you can compartmentalize your feelings and truly come across as fine. As far as anyone else in the world knows, you are defined by the letters you type in your profile.

But what about body language?

What about tone of voice?

What about those times when you can communicate with various other vehicles to let someone know you need a little more connection than the rhetorical "How are you doing?"

You can see the implications piling up quite fast as dating relationships become much more complicated. But the fact of the matter is, social-networking sites have redefined how we develop relationships today.

A teenager in Southern California confessed to me not long ago that dating at his school is a culmination of texting between classes. A guy might see a girl he is attracted to, send a text that identifies a time and a place to meet, and the physical relationship begins. If all goes well, then going out on a date might happen, but only if both allow those compartments to bleed over into a real-life personal journey.

This can make dating a tricky topic to pin down, as the definition has so drastically changed over the last several years. It's not the same era as when people were who they were all the time. This generation of students has the ability to stack their lives up in different compartments, to almost make a multiple-level personality that is very dangerous. Everything we've known about dating up to this point in time we must be willing to put on the table of ideas and begin to understand a multi-level personality in every person.

Some authors refer to this phenomenon as the dualistic generation, but I would propose the term *dualistic* is an extremely naive word. Teenagers today live *multiple* personalities. Relationships exist at so many levels and compartments in their lives that we have to deconstruct those barriers in order to get down to the issues at hand.

Recently I was sitting with a teenage friend.

We've talked of dating, marriage, commitment, and purity for the last five years.

She knows what I think about dating and saving yourself for marriage.

We were eating at a local restaurant with several others, and in the middle of the meal she announced, "I'm having a baby!"

Unsolicited.

Not a part of the conversation.

She just threw it out there.

You can imagine my shock in the moment. I had no idea. I was totally caught off guard. My mind went into hyperdrive. *How in the world could this happen? Here is a girl with all the tools to keep her dating relationship pure, yet she has become another statistic. She is now another teenage pregnancy. How? Why? And what can I do to help future generations from having to face the same issues?*

Evidently everyone else at the table had gotten the memo, but I was clueless and had no idea.

I almost choked on my delicious lettuce wrap, and I looked at her with what must have been the biggest surprised eyes she'd ever seen.

"Excuse me?" I finally asked.

"Yeah, so I'm having a baby in March, and I thought you ought to know."

"Uhhhh . . . WOW!"

I had only a few seconds to compose myself because I wanted to make sure she knew I loved her and supported her for who she was. I didn't want to be that guy who teenagers are afraid to tell their problems to, so I just started asking questions.

"Who's the dad?"

"When did you find out?"

"How far along are you?"

As she answered, some things started becoming even clearer. My friend, who was now pregnant, was treating this pregnancy like a speed bump on the road of life. She was going to continue school, get a job after the baby was born, and just pick right up from where she left off.

I sat amazed at the disconnect. "This is going to change your whole life," I said.

"I know, but I have a lot of help. I think I can keep going," she quickly retorted.

I am happy to say that she gave birth to a beautiful baby boy. Mom and baby are healthy and happy, and she does have a wonderful family foundation to help her raise her son. But while I was sitting there in the restaurant with our friends, it felt like she hadn't even considered the reality of her decision.

Obviously, my response was one of great concern and care. We walked down the crowded downtown streets for a long time. We laughed. We cried. And at the end of our conversation, I told her I was going to support her any way she needed. But the fact remained: Here was a close friend I'd taught for a long time, but somehow I hadn't been speaking her language.

THE SECRETS THEY KEEP

Twenty years ago I started my pursuit of acting in my hometown of Little Rock, Arkansas. I signed up with an agency, took some photos, and started auditioning for local advertisements. It was a fun hobby for a while, but eventually it turned into my undergraduate focus. I love the theater. I love acting. I love art. I love the way you can express ideas and feelings through simplistic creative processes.

Until I went into theater full time, homosexuality was something out "there." It was a group of people who were trying to tear apart the Judeo-Christian values of America, and we had to be on the lookout for "those" people. Until I went to college, I never met anyone who claimed even one iota of a same-sex alternative lifestyle.

However, when I got to college, my world changed dramatically. Students were struggling to know who they were, how they were made, and to whom they were attracted. A cloud of uncertainty hung over much of the population. Sure, there was still the normal frat-guy mentality, but a lot of people were trying to figure out if they were straight or gay.

In my book *Love This!*[2] I share a specific story of how Christians can learn to deal with the homosexual agenda, so I won't go into a lot of detail in this book. However, there is a part of teenage dating that we need to be aware of: mainly same-sex attraction.

Was I Born This Way? Because I Sure Didn't Choose to Be . . .

Most of the kids I work with who struggle with same-sex attraction are male (but that doesn't mean girls aren't dealing with this just the same).

A few years ago, I met a wonderful counselor who specialized in same-sex addiction. His whole practice was set up to help people who were addicted to pornography, strange sexual behavior, or same-sex addiction. We sat across the table at a national conference, and I was intrigued by the way he explained the issues boys deal with when they go through the sexual development process.

Parents, LISTEN TO THIS!

There is absolutely no evidence to date to point out a gene in the human body that genetically predisposes someone to a homosexual lifestyle. It would be a great scientific discovery to put an end to that debate, but the fact of the matter is, at this point, we know of zero reasons someone is biologically homosexual.

So that must mean they are all living in sin, right?

WRONG!

Homosexuality isn't a biological issue, and it's not something someone chooses to be in life. Just ask any of your homosexual acquaintances what they think about the possibility of being born gay. Almost every student I counsel struggles with the idea that a loving God would make them this way. They endure a tremendous amount of pressure, scrutiny, and confusion. It's not until homosexual men and women reach adulthood and are able to solidify their identity that they try to come to terms with it. In the meantime, they're trying to convince themselves and others that it's just a normal way of life. (Mind you, if you encounter a homosexual who believes in Darwinian evolution, it's a different matter altogether. For how can genes pass from one generation to the next without procreation? But I digress.)

I have been in several sessions working with guys who are confused about sexual orientation, and I've found some interesting correlations I think might help us navigate as we have more and more students asking hard questions. In my research there are five different issues male teenagers struggle with when they are working through the homosexuality issue:

1. Affirmation. We all desire affirmation, and our developmental process requires it. We must have a place where we find emotional security, and most of the time that is found in a father figure. If guys don't receive affirmation from a man as they navigate their emotional growth, then when they go through the cosmic clash called puberty, they long for that kind of affirmation—but it gets confused in the rise of sexual hormones. All of a sudden a young boy begins to search for emotional affirmation through a sexual lens.

2. Feminine Characteristics. I was always interested in why the arts—includingthe music industry, the fashion industry, art museum groups, dancers, and especially actors—attract a large portion of the homosexual community. There is a large population of homosexuals in those groups. Why? Where are the straight creatives?

Our society labels kids early on. If they're interested in music instead of football, some families use homosexual slang to identify them. If they want to make clothes instead of build buildings, kids on the playground start using terms like *gay* (or whatever awful term is popular in school at the time).

Just because someone is born with more culturally effeminate characteristics has nothing to do with whether or not he is gay or straight. But how long does it take before name-calling convinces someone of their identity? Much of the time teens are just trying to be normal in a masculine society.

3. Early Sexuality. Many teenagers struggling with homosexual identity issues have been exposed to pornography before puberty. I was talking with a student not long ago, and he told me EVERY BOY AT SCHOOL is into porn.

"Really? *Everybody* is a large percentage," I countered.

"EVERY BOY," he insisted.

It's no wonder teenage boys are struggling to figure out who they are sexually when all around them are fantasy-type sexual encounters in movies or magazines and on the Internet. Early exposure to sexuality sets the brain on a course of confusion. We need to fight to protect our kids from this evil plaguing our society today. Pornography might be more dangerous than terrorists, obesity, or any other social ill today. It's extremely damaging to the early development of the brain.

4. Abuse. More and more kids are telling me stories of sexual abuse in their family. Uncles, brothers, fathers, and friends make up a deviant group of sexual misfits who are preying on our young. It's not uncommon for me to see 60 to 70 percent of the kids I talk with have a history with some sort of sexual abuse. Parents and leaders, you must understand that early abuse to a child requires a long road to recovery. The synapses that help us understand our sentient sexual personhood are derailed if we are exposed to sexual abuse early on. Most guys struggling with same-sex attraction have endured some kind of sexual predatory abuse, and it breaks my heart. This isn't how God created the world to be.

5. A House of Cards. This is where the details come together. Homosexuality definitely isn't a biological choice, and it certainly isn't a selfish choice for a lifestyle of sin. Some boys have been dealt one, two, or all of these "cards" (and there are several more indicators). The hand they hold at life's poker table has little to do with their choosing and more to do with the cards they were dealt in life.

So instead of pointing your finger at the homosexual community and damning them to hell for some sin they commit, we need to embrace a paradigm shift where we help guide students in their own sexual development. We need to be the ones talking with teens about sex. We need to be the ones dealing with the tragedy of abuse. We need to train them to guard their minds so they don't become lured into the world of porn. We need to be the ones sharing with them the ultimate design for sexuality as God created it.

We certainly don't need any more "God Hates Gays" posters on the news. We need people who love unconditionally. We need a church that can welcome everyone with open arms. We need a process where we can help those who want help — and offer it unconditionally.

If the world saw Christians opening their arms to people dealing with obvious sexual issues, they might get a clearer picture of how God extends His love to sinners — unconditionally.

I believe we must realign our dating discussions.

We must go back to the drawing board in our talks about relationships and sexuality.

We can't rely on purity rings, rallies, and small-group discussions.

We must be willing to live life *with* our kids, not *at* them.

If we are willing to listen to the problems teens are dealing with, then we'll have a much easier time identifying the solutions they need — rather than the solutions we think they need.

CHAPTER 5

MARRIAGE

WHY SHOULD TEENAGERS be concerned about a marriage relationship?

I'm not sure many parents and youth leaders today understand what teens think about marriage. After decades of the divorce plague in our society, many teens are left asking, "Why?"

Why should they get married?

Ask Christian teenagers today why they should get married, and ultimately you'll wind up hearing, "Well, marriage is the ticket to sex, right?"

Sex?

That's all marriage is about?

You can't blame them.

That's all we've told them. Sex. Marriage. Marriage. Sex. There's no real understanding of sexuality as a creation of God. There's little understanding that marriage is a committed relationship between two people. Sex. That's it.

Now don't get me wrong; sex is a crucial component of a marriage, but it certainly isn't the culmination of everything married. So why? If I can physically have sex outside of marriage, why do I need marriage?

You can find varying statistical information on marriage and divorce, but most of the surveys point to the disparaging fact that Christian marriages divorce at the same rate as non-Christian marriages, according to the Smalley Relationship Center.[1] So what's the point?

If we're going to get married just to get divorced, let's save everybody the trouble and pain, and just live together. That's what teens today are thinking.

EXPECTATIONS

Of course, most teen girls still think there is a knight in shining armor waiting to ride them into the sunset fairy tale, but maybe that's the problem.

The expectations put on marriage today are totally unrealistic. It's like the American dream drifted into our perception of marriage. We've watched too many movies where love wins out every time and things work out in the end. We need to be sure we paint realistic expectations for students today so they can be ready to face the "real world."[2]

It's time we're honest with teens and college students about marriage. It's not a Disney story. Marriage rarely takes the narrative of *Cinderella* or *The Princess and the Frog*.

Sure, marriage is about romance.

It's about Valentine's Days with flowers and hearts.

It's about birthdays.

It's about sexy getaway weekends to connect with each other.

Sometimes.

But let's be honest: Marriage is about love and commitment. It's about sharing life together, the good times *and* the bad.

Marriage is about going out with someone you find super-attractive, waking up to someone with bedhead and running makeup, and *still* choosing to love that person.

SO HOW?

I've watched for the last several years as the TWILIGHT series has taken the world by storm. Not since the Harry Potter epidemic has our culture been so enamored with reading and story. I was at our local bookstore a few years ago, saw the series on a bookshelf, and innocently asked, "So, what is *Twilight*?"

Good thing I had some time.

I stood there for almost twenty minutes as a lady went on and on about the story of vampires and werewolves. I was so disgusted with her explanation. I thought, *I've gotta read this for myself.* So I bought the first book and started in.

What an interesting concept. The TWILIGHT series actually captures the loneliness of today's high school kids. Bella, a typical American high schooler, is introduced to a vampire named Edward, who has chosen to be a "vegetarian" vampire, so to speak. Um, okay . . . so he doesn't eat people; rather he lives on the blood of animals.

When the girl senses something mysterious about her vampire friend, he keeps the secret a bit longer (natural tension).

Without rewriting the entire series here, suffice it to say that I believe our teenage culture is consumed with a TWILIGHT type of dating. Girls expect guys to have a hunger for them. Guys expect girls to fall in love with the introduction of mystery. It's a setup. There's no vampire on the planet who can compete with the kind of desire Edward has for Bella.

The vehicle is quite impressive, and to its merit, the story is one of abstinence — but it's done nothing to encourage today's teenagers about how to date in reality. It's just another way we've thrown unrealistic expectations about love and marriage at the modern American teen.

So the onset of *Twilight* brings us to another question: How can we prepare teenagers and college students for the reality of marriage and commitment? *For real!*

How can we help them see that relationships have a lot to do with romance, but there's a whole suitcase full of other relational clothing we all have to wear?

Love

I think we need to redefine the concept of love, don't you?

I love my dog.

I love my car.

I love Mexican food.

I love my wife.

What? What's up with that?

Love isn't a word that we can flippantly throw around and expect students to understand what we're talking about. We've got to help them understand the realities of love.

Love can't be reduced to the latest romantic comedy.

Certainly the hormonal feelings that happen during teenage pubescent growth can't be love.

Love isn't making out in the shadowy corners of the local high school.

So what is it?

The Bible says it like this:

> Love is patient, love is kind. It does not envy, it does not boast, it is not proud. It is not rude, it is not self-seeking, it is not easily angered, it keeps no record of wrongs. Love does not delight in evil but rejoices with the truth. It always protects, always trusts, always hopes, always perseveres. Love never fails. (1 Corinthians 13:4-8)

Can you see it? Can you see the golden thread of truth woven in and out of the most popular love chapter in the Scriptures?

Love is patient. What does our world tell us about patience?

Love is kind. What does our culture tell us about the value of being kind?

Love does not envy or boast.

Love is not proud.

Do you see it?

Love, at the very core of its being, is *selfless*. It's self-sacrificing. It thinks more about the person receiving than the one giving. At the core of knowing, *love is sacrifice.*

Think about it.

God is Love.

What is God's ultimate display of His own character?

Romans 5:8 says, "While we were still sinners, Christ died for us."

If God is love, and the ultimate display of His affection was to come and sacrifice Himself for the world (see John 3:16), then it's pretty easy to correlate love to sacrifice.

So how do we know we're in love? I'll tell you.

Jamie Jo and I have a wonderful relationship. We have to be in love, or we wouldn't have lasted as long as we have already. So how do I know I love her?

I know I love my wife because I choose to think the best of her. I have a special highlight reel that plays in my mind as I think about her. I don't hold her faults against her. I don't think about the bad things. I choose to sacrifice my right to hold things against her, for the sake of the good times.

For example . . .

I'm way into road biking. There's nothing else in the world that brings the kind of therapy to me as riding my bike on the road on a warm summer day. So I thought, *Hey, if I bought my wife a road bike, maybe we could enjoy it together, right*? Seemed like a great idea at the time.

We went down to the local bike store. Found a bike she liked. We picked it out and rolled out of the store with thoughts of long rides together out in the mountains where we live. As I walked up to the car, I noticed I was going to need a bike rack because our car didn't have the room needed to hold a bike. So we strolled back into the shop and bought a beautiful Thule bike rack for our car.

I couldn't believe it. Not only was I married to this beautiful woman, but she was now geared up and outfitted to be a road biker. How could I ask for anything more?

We got the bike adjusted on top of the car.

And we drove off into the future of many, many rides together as a couple.

It was about a week later when I got the phone call: "Honey, um, I have some bad news."

Evidently she had loaned the bike out to one of our friends. When he came back, he forgot the bike was on top of the car and tried to park in the garage. In doing so he ripped the frame of the bike in half.

I can only say anger is an understatement.

Why didn't she do something to help remind the guy not to drive into the garage?

Why didn't she take more care of her bike?

Why did she loan it out in the first place?

I know, for some it might seem like a minor deal, but it was something I was really excited about.

But it didn't do any good to rant and rave.

Getting mad at her wasn't going to fix the bike.

At that moment I could choose to be really angry and give in to my own selfish feelings, *or* I could choose to love and forgive.

I chose the second.

I chose to think about my wife's good qualities. She wanted to spend time with me. She was willing to ride her bike down the road. She was excited and interested in my hobby. It was awesome! I choose to think good things.

That's love.

Love is sacrifice for someone else.

It's choosing to see the good in someone.

It's not just a lovey-dovey feeling you get; it's a choice to wake up every day and make a personal commitment to sacrifice your own desires for the one you love.

It's not like loving a pizza.

It's not the same as loving a car.

True love is something we can help students embrace through the choice of sacrifice.

Sex

There are way too many True Love Waits rallies.

They don't work.

Teenage sexual activity is the same within the church as it is outside the church.

There's no difference, and the reason is . . .

Teenagers have the ability to compartmentalize everything in their existence.

Imagine walking into a mighty castle during the days of old. Hallways go on for miles and miles. Doorways lead to secret locations. Escape routes, dungeons, and the occasional secret passageway make up a maze of possible choices.

That's the mind of a teenager today.

It's a complex structure, full of doors blocking the way in and out of certain areas of life.

One door might lead to their sports life while another leads directly to spiritual understanding.

One secret passage might unveil the reason they choose the friends they do, and still another will lead you to their opinion on sexuality.

The crazy door to sexuality can even have a couple of different entryways.

For example, you might find a teenager who truly believes in his heart he wants to wait to have sex before marriage, but you find out through another passageway, he's already sexually active with his girlfriend.

You can see the challenge we face, right?

We must be able to navigate the hallways of their hearts, all the while understanding that compartmentalization can hide the truth. And what's more, they don't have any reason to believe the disconnection from one to the other is wrong.

So you can literally have a purity rally on Friday night, invite students to pledge their celibacy till marriage, and leave with everyone on the same page. Then on Saturday night, they'll be out partying with their friends, engaged in the same activities they pledged to stay away from only an evening before.

Character

I know it doesn't make sense, but as I've traveled the globe, I've learned that Western teenagers are able to compartmentalize every area of their lives — which is exactly why we have to take time teaching students comprehensive worldview principles.

They need to understand that their character isn't just defined by what pictures they choose to put up on Facebook or MySpace. Rather, their character is defined by what they believe at their core level of existence, and their behavior is merely an extension of what they believe.

It's why I think a solid comprehensive worldview curriculum is essential for teenagers today. They need to see what consequences of ideas really are. They need to understand the inconsistencies of conflicting worldviews as they try to live an honest and authentic life.

If your teens or students don't know what a worldview is before they go off to college, you've done them a great disservice. We need to educate our kids in what it means to believe in God and the commitment we have to understanding and following God as we believe.

As parents and youth leaders, we need to be committed to a comprehensive Christian worldview development program. There are schools, camps, books, and online programs that can help equip you to talk to your teens about sexuality. But without the comprehensive nature, I'm afraid you'll just be putting the information together piecemeal. We must start with God and why we believe in Him, and then we can help them see the how-tos.

Commitment

I recently interviewed a student who revealed the "dating scene" at her school. She explained that relationships typically begin with lewd text messages that eventually lead two people to a location to make out. If the make-out session goes well, then the relationship might move forward, but if there were issues on either side, it ends right there in the dark shadows of secrecy.

It's almost like we are watching teenagers riding an amusement park ride at Disney rather than finding out how to relate to one another in a dating relationship. I watch and listen as they describe their relationship like a roller coaster. As soon as the ride ends, it's time to get off and find a new ride.

It's no surprise that we have commitment issues at the teenage level.

It's no surprise that as they grow into adults, they have no idea what it means to think of lifelong marriage relationships.

It's not their fault, really.

We complain about the destruction of marriage, but adults aren't doing anything to curb the problem. Sure, they have weekend marriage seminars. There are stories where marriages bent on failing were saved for a short time because of a reconnect, but go to a high school assembly and just ask. Ask for everyone who comes from a divorced home to raise their hands. You'll be shocked.

When was the last time you met a couple that had been married for more than thirty years?

Most likely it's someone born in the 1920s or 1930s. Have you ever asked why? (I assure you it's not just because they're old enough to be married that long.) Why was the "greatest generation," as Tom Brokaw wrote in his book, the only generation that could stay together?

Is it because younger generations don't know how to love?

Is it because our definition of *love* is some ooey-gooey feeling?

Is it because we don't know commitment?

Or could it be that we don't do a very good job of preparing kids to enter in to the sanctity of marriage?

One of my closest friends works on the "gay marriage" agenda issue in his home state. They have several rallies, education seminars, and get-the-word-out type events to stop gay marriage from coming to his state.

I admire him greatly for the work he does, but I'm a bit perplexed by the people who are willing to protest it. The cry "Don't change the definition of marriage" rings out loud and clear, but what does that mean? A man and a woman? Okay, I get that. But how can we stand for the sanctity of marriage in our culture when all we do is use marriage for a temporary relationship? We're doing more to destroy marriage than the gay rights groups ever proposed.

(Again, a topic for another book.)

The fact of the matter is, students are growing up in an environment that propagates this "married till I'm finished" culture. When I ask youth to raise their hands to show divorce in their homes, in almost every teenage group I speak to more than half of them raise their hands. It doesn't matter if it's a secular school group or a Christian youth gathering; the amount of divorce in the lives of teenagers is staggering.

So how can we expect them to rise up and do anything different?

The model of marriage they see in our society simply uses marriage as long as it feels right, but when it's time to move on, move on.

Youth leaders around the country need to be clear on marriage.

What is it?

How long does it last?

What does it mean to commit your life to one another?

Who are the models of a committed relationship for today's teens?

The best models for me were my parents and my youth directors. They showed me the good times and the hard times. I remember watching my youth directors hold hands with their spouses. I remember seeing my parents try to work out hard arguments. I was privy to the fact that marriage was more than a license to have sex in a Christian community. I knew that it was a commitment, that there was sacrifice to be made.

THE MODELING FACTOR

Rules without relationships lead to rebellion.

—JOSH McDOWELL

Ideas have consequences.

I recently watched an impressive documentary on the nature of sexuality inside a specific religious denomination. It wasn't anything new; it just put real faces with the stories I've heard about sexual atrocities that happen all over the world.

This particular film introduced the idea that homosexuality is a sin.

Now, no matter what you think about homosexuality, the initial idea that homosexuality is a sin leads us to consequences. A statement like that generates real-life consequences that, when taken to its full reality, can be abhorred.

Think about that for a minute.

What kind of consequences do we live by when we identify a certain lifestyle as a sin?

Some might say, "Well, we need to make sure *those* people aren't around my kids." So we introduce the abandonment of a specific group.

Others will say, "They have a disease that needs to be cured." So we introduce medications that will help cure this disease from a biomechanical process.

Still others might say, "It's an emotional problem in the brain, and they need to be fixed." So someone takes on the issue and comes up with a specific psychoanalytical treatment.

As I watched this denomination begin to identify treatment programs for people to be healed, I saw the most egregious torture mechanism sanctioned by a church that I've ever seen.

Men were hooked up to electrodes and forced to watch pictures of naked men. Every time they felt aroused, they had to hit a button that forced a charge to go through their bodies. The idea likened itself to Pavlov's dog experiment as the church tried to adhere to universal rules. If only we can induce pain in a situation that would normally cause arousal, we could cure these poor diseased people.

I watched the documentarian walk through halls of mental facilities where homosexual people were quarantined from the rest of society as they were thought to be able to infect the rest of the population. Isolation became the consequence of dealing with a rule, and all of this was sanctioned and funded by the church.

He even went so far as to show actual experimental lobotomies where the frontal lobes of people's brains were removed in order to control their emotional neurology and curb their desire to be gay. *All sanctioned by the church!*

Are you catching the point here?

The "rule" from the church results in actual consequences in the lives of real people. Remember, it's not about whether or not homosexuality is sinful, at least for this discussion. It made me think of Josh McDowell's comment, "Rules without relationships lead to rebellion."[3]

At the end of the obviously pro-homosexual film, I watched the real pain brought to life as people tried to tell the stories of how they were treated. There had been no *relationships* made. There were no focus groups to talk through the issues. There was absolutely *no* education about how someone might come to be gay. Pure and simple, homosexuality was a disorder of the human condition that needed to be fixed.

The same concept rings true when churches, families, and other organizations point to "sex before marriage is a sin." Whether or not the statement is true doesn't matter to this generation. They are feeling the consequences of sanctioned alienation and brutal dictatorial rules without any form of relationship to help them understand why or how.

It's in our own homes, isn't it? Rules about sexuality at home without the relationship to reinforce those rules are driving teenagers to rebellion in their own sexuality. They hear a mom or a dad mandate how they should live out their God-given sexuality, and often they don't have any sort of reference or model to reference.

Remember, teenagers today are less concerned with informational content. In fact, truth to the modern-day teenager is only true if it is experienced and modeled as a real solution in real life. They've tied so much of experience to the facts and nature of life that even today's view of sexuality has been compromised to whatever feels good. And why not?

Why is homosexuality wrong?

Why is sex before marriage a bad thing?

Who is modeling a "right" way of living out their sexuality without sensualizing, capitalizing, or presenting some illicit form of sex in the modern world?

Teenagers are witnessing one of the largest breakdowns of the family in modern times. Divorce rates continue to hover above 50 percent, and the idea that sexuality demands long-term commitment is something of an old, worn-out system. Either cognitively or intuitively, teens watch the trends of couples today and come up with their own system. It's almost like watching the novel *Lord of the Flies* play out in real life.

If there is no modeling that goes on to help teens see a productive, successful sexual relationship, then it's no wonder they would try to come up with a system that works for them in their time. They tend to look at their parents and the failures of the system they so tried to hold on to, and they see a broken set of rules. No one wants to show up on their wedding day with the idea that someday they'll have to endure a long, grueling divorce, but that's exactly what's happening.

Marriage has become a sort of suggestion rather than "till death do us part."

Now that's not to say there aren't mistakes. I'm not advocating that we need a society of perfection to turn the tide of teenage sexuality. But what I am asking for are real-life models who have a form of commitment that invigorates a lively sexual relationship.

What we have today is a system whereby a church, small group, or parachurch ministry might say, "Don't have sex before you get married — it's wrong," and all teens hear are rules and regulations. Whether or not there is an objective truth claim, they'll see it as subjective until they have real-life models who prove the rule is worth something.

We can't continue to beat the drum of abstinence if we're not also willing to practice "till death do us part," model lifelong monogamy, and openly discuss the consequences in relationships where those commitments are not valued.

We have teens who are being quarantined because they're just doing what they see modeled in society. We watch as teenagers are overridden with guilt when they follow exactly what their elders have modeled. The sad stories I hear from students *all the time* break my heart, not because they messed up sexually but because of the undue burden placed on them as outcasts to their spiritual organization. And why?

I think it happens because we're not showing them a model of true biblically based sexual lives. God created sexuality as a part of who we are. It drives us. It is such an important part of development. In fact, it's the sole proponent of the human race. To merely create rules surrounding it, without the proper understanding of relationship, is only to awaken a heart of rebellion and an attitude sick with hypocrisy.

I recently read an article about the number of teenagers and college students who've decided to live together before they get married. It would blow your mind. The idea that more and more students are taking the position "It's better to live together than get divorced" begins to fracture the very foundation of the sanctity of marriage. But who can blame them? I mean, if you take a short look at the last five years of marriage in our country alone, it's almost logical for kids to take that position.

You can make rules.

You can try to regulate the behavior of your teens.

You can preach till you're blue in the face.

But until we take the courageous stand to walk with kids through the formative years of sexuality, how can we expect anything to change?

Every time I address students on the topic of marriage and sexuality, I want to be sure they get the whole story. I want to make sure they see the inside of my own life.

I tell of my romantic stories with Jamie Jo.

I walk them through what it looks like to date properly.

I try to explain that sex is more about the emotional state of the relationship than even the physical pleasure it brings.

But I'm also quick to point out the failures in my life.

I tell them how I messed up with girls in high school.

I tell them how my relationships in college have been detrimental to my marriage life and the trust factor between Jamie Jo and me.

I'm honest with them. I openly admit that marriage isn't like the latest Disney movie, but it *is* the most rewarding time of connection you will have with any other human on the planet.

And you know what?

They *listen*.

More and more teenagers are willing to digest the successes and failures and develop an idea of marriage that is more true to reality than the pictures Hollywood tries to paint.

They see the vulnerability of a human relationship bound by commitment, and they find comfort in knowing that when they struggle with sexuality, they're not alone. They're more willing to think and talk through the issues if they know that thinking those things and saying those things won't make them a weirdo, won't ostracize them from the world. And only by thinking and talking through the issues can they land at rational decisions and concrete concepts that resonate with their realities.

I've walked with so many students through an honest journey of the whys and hows that I truly believe there will be more realistic expectations going into the future. It's not good enough just to tell kids what to believe today. We've got to recapture the days where there are real-life examples that work in real time.

Modeling is key!

Again, if dating is reduced to a physical relationship, then I'm out. I'm not going to advocate a process of relationship building that takes kids further away from the truth of togetherness. *But* . . . if we can begin teaching kids—through our own actions, our own lives—how to communicate, how to be problem solvers, how to be sacrificial lovers, then I'm in.

PART II

THE WAY TO DATE

CHAPTER 6

PARENTAL INVOLVEMENT

ASIDE FROM MODELING great relationships, how much should parents be involved in teaching students how to date?

I can remember back in junior high, looking at a girl who had started looking at me. It was more than the "Will you go with me?" of the third grade. No, this was "true love."

Of course, my parents were worried.

What kind of girl is hunting my son?

How do I protect his heart?

When should I talk to him about sexuality?

And how?

(By the way, I'd like to take a second here to inject a little issue all parents need to take into consideration. If your child is above the age of thirteen, *he or she knows about sex*. No parents are good enough to shield their kids from the world like that. So just put that arrow in your quiver, and we'll talk more about that later.)

Back to the junior high story . . .

I remember going on youth-group outings with my church and

having an aching in my heart to be with this girl, and my parents were wondering how in the world they were going to navigate this seeming pitfall in their son's life.

KEYS TO NAVIGATING DATING

Being a youth leader now, I get it.

I get the pressure on both sides.

On the teenage side, I understand the need to be with someone.

But I understand that my kids are entering a dating age.

I feel a responsibility to protect them from all the bad stuff the world is throwing at them.

How can anyone possibly figure out how to sail this ship?

Here are a few ways I've helped parents and youth leaders to be involved in teen dating relationships:

1. Be ready to accept them for who they are.

One of the hardest issues parents have to deal with is growth and change in their kid's life.

There is a natural "growing up" that has to happen before our kids can go off and make their own choices, become good citizens, and handle the pressures of their own careers, families, hobbies, and spiritual investments.

The problem with some families happens when either Mom or Dad forgets the natural process. We have visions of those little boys climbing in our laps, needing our every minute of attention. We have dreams of those little girls looking deep into our eyes and saying, "Daddy." And let's be honest, we're scared those days are coming to an end. We fear change. We fear the consequential fact that we're getting older. We fear we'll never have the chance to relive those moments. And you know what? We have every right to fear.

But God didn't give us a spirit of fear.

And it's not our responsibility to keep our kids needy.

They need to be raised to make their own decisions.

They need to understand the pain of failure.

They need to celebrate the mountaintops of success.

They need to have mentors and coaches they know will believe in them, no matter what.

Out of fear, parents and youth leaders often hijack their relationship with teens and students by coming across as more concerned with losing their position of authority than strengthening their position as a mentor.

If you're going to speak into a teenager's life concerning dating, you must recognize that they are on a journey from childhood into a place of adulthood. Every day is a day closer to a place where they can make their own decisions. Every day the little girl is transforming into a beautiful woman. Every day that little boy is turning into a handsome man, and we must prepare them, especially concerning dating.

It's a common technique in coaching to fill the hearts of your players, so that when you need to correct them, they'll actually listen.

My high school coach was a genius when it came to motivating. He didn't just turn it on at game time. He didn't just ride us hard in practice. He spent Monday nights opening up his home for us to do a Bible study. He had open office hours when the players could come and talk about whatever they wanted to talk about. He took his job seriously. It was more than just the game.

Parents and leaders, we need to see kids growing up as more than a game. We can't expect to speak into their dating lives only when it's time for them to walk out the door on a date. We have to build a rapport with our kids so that when dating becomes the issue, they'll listen.

Not because we say, "I'm the dad (or leader), so there." But rather, they'll listen because they know we want the best for them. (And as an added bonus, if we're modeling healthy relationships, they'll know that we know what we're talking about.) We want them to live a successful life of relationships.

If you're interested in coaching a teenager about dating, you've got to strengthen your relationship with him or her *now*. You can't just wait for the homecoming dance or the prom to start working on this concept. It takes a lot of time and investment.

So how? How do you start building confidence in your teenager today?

2. Make sure you have a healthy relationship with your teen or student.

A mentor of mine once told me to think of friendship like a bank account. It feels great to put money in and watch the numbers continue to climb, but it really hurts to pull money out. You don't want to take money away from your savings unless it's absolutely necessary.

Relationships with our kids aren't that different.

Think of the currency of relationships like this:

Encouragement = Money in the Bank
Compassion = Money in the Bank
Time Doing Something Your Teen or Student Enjoys = Deposit

But . . .

Discipline = Withdrawal
Accountability = Money Going Out
Raising Your Voice = Void

When you add up all the times you spend with your teenager, you want to make sure your encouraging times *always* outweigh your discipline times in the same way you always want your checking account positive. It gives you the platform to be a leader, a mentor, and a friend.

I realize you're called to be the parent (or leader).

I know there are some arenas where you won't have a choice but to lay down the law.

But make sure you're also spending time on the other end of the ledger.

Teenagers aren't that different from adults.

They long to know that people care for them.

They want to have people they can count on.

They're interested in participating in life with people.

And they *need* clear direction.

My son is at the age where he's getting ready to enter into dating relationships. So, right now, I'm camping with him, playing video games with him, reading with him, building with him, and trying to establish a bank account that can withstand the times when I'm going to have to sit him down and say tough things.

In fact, just the other day I took my son down to the river outside our place here in Colorado. I'm an amateur fly fisherman, and I thought it was time to teach him how to fish.

We went down to the river in anxious anticipation of catching the big one.

We spent a little while working on casting.

I taught him what a fly fishing fly really looked like.

We picked out our fly and started fishing.

Five minutes into our fishing outing, the bite came, and my son had a fish on the line.

We pulled, reeled, let out the line, and worked the drag, and in no time at all we had a twenty-two-inch cutthroat trout on the end of the line. I wish you could have seen his face. He caught his first fish, and it was a monster.

The event was the first part of the memory, but now he tells that story to all of my friends. "Hey, my dad and I went down to the river and caught this *huge* cutthroat trout."

When my friends hear how big it was, they all look at me like,

"Are you kidding me? Who is this kid?"

And the smile on his face radiates. He knows he did something special, and the memory we made is paying dividends every day.

Being a parent is tough, especially when you're trying to man the ship of a teenage dating life. It's not as easy as just saying, "Do this" or "Do that." Relationships take work, and it means so much more to a teenager that you care about them than it does that you're trying to coach them through their own hormonal life. Understanding the heart and mind of a teenager just takes time. It takes intentional time that you are investing.

As you begin talking to your teenager about dating, be sure your bank account is full. We all know dating, sex, and relationships can be touchy subjects, but if they trust you, it can be the most exciting adventure you've traveled together yet.

3. Be prepared to set some boundaries.

After you're sure your bank account has enough currency for a with-drawal, you've got the right to set down the rules. You're the parent, and it's your responsibility to protect and guide. I know it seems a little strange to follow such an ooey-gooey relationship section with a rules section, but we've got to have standards and boundaries. They add structure to the ooey-gooey.

If we're going to teach our students how to date, then we need to make sure they understand that it's a learning process.

I remember teaching my oldest son how to ride a bicycle. We started with the training wheels, and I pushed from behind. Slowly, as he grew enough confidence and got the feel of the bike, I took the training wheels off. After pushing, I'd let go a bit. He'd fall down, and then we'd get back on and try again.

Teaching a teen to date isn't that different.

As you gain trust by keeping the emotional bank account full, these simple guidelines for dating won't seem weird or out of bounds. Rather, teenagers will begin seeing opportunity for you to be involved in their dating lives.

Meeting the date is essential.

You have the right to know whom your son or daughter is going to spend an evening with. Make sure you set the standard for meeting your teen's date before they go out. No exceptions.

As with riding a bike, if your teen is going to ease into a dating relationship, start slowly. Say your son or daughter is interested in going out with a special friend from school. Invite them along for a fishing session or take them shopping with you. Go to the mall for a snack, and spend some time getting to know them. Don't make it seem like an interview; just try to get to know who this person is, their likes and dislikes, how they interact with your teenager, what they participate in at school and church. You'll be the coolest person in school, and the kids will start seeing you as someone they can begin to trust. That's the training wheels.

As you see an opportunity, suggest they go out for pizza together or give them other opportunities to ensure that you can begin to trust them. Trust is earned, and when kids feel like they have an opportunity to earn trust, they rise to the challenge and rarely abuse it.

But if they feel like they are getting away with something, they'll push the boundaries. They'll try to sneak out if they feel like they have to. Don't take the training wheels off too soon, but give them the chance to see what it's like to ride the bike without you around every now and then.

If any boy wants to date my daughter and thinks he can just honk in the driveway for her to come outside, he'd better keep on driving. We're not a honk-and-drive family. I want to sit down with the people my teenagers are spending time with. I want to know what they're thinking. I want to know how they process information. I want to be able to trust them, so I'm going to give them every opportunity to earn my trust.

Setting a curfew: It's up to you.

Kids complain all the time about so-and-so's mom who lets them stay out later. Teenagers don't mind a curfew as long as it's not ridiculous. Let's be honest: How much good happens after midnight anyway?

When I was in college, the biggest fights I had with Jamie Jo *always* happened after midnight. It's just the nature of getting tired, winding down from the day, and being bored. Try to help your teenager understand you're setting boundaries for their own safety.

Just keep asking, "What good happens after midnight?"

It's a great idea to contact the family of the person your son or daughter is dating and sit down for a little context meeting. If you can tackle it together, the curfew thing becomes less of a big deal. Everyone knows if Johnny has to be in by ten, then Sally needs to be in at the same time (or *before* if he's bringing her home). It just makes it easier to lay down the law if you need to.

Again, I wouldn't imagine letting my teenage son or daughter hang out till the wee hours of the morning. *Nothing good happens after midnight* in the teenage world. Just trust me on this one.

Reading text messages: Do it.

I can call a teenager on his cell phone, and he may not answer. I can text the same teenager only seconds later, and I'll get a text right back.

What in the world? I understand there are times when you can't pick up the phone, but for this generation texting has become the preferred method over talking on the phone. Texting is just the way teenagers communicate today, which is a benefit because we can see a log of communication for the whole day.

If I were you, I'd be taking opportunities to read through your kid's text messages. I know that sounds intrusive, but the things teenagers will share on the screen of a cell phone is increasingly more honest than what they'll say to you or even their friends in person. The face of a cell phone is ambiguous; it's not personal. Your teenager's deepest secrets can be found in their text log. You can find out a lot about what's going on at school by taking a peek every now and again.

And let's not forget the epidemic of sexting.

I know you don't think your teens will ever do anything like this, but it's happening at an unprecedented level. In our sex-driven society, teens are becoming more and more visual. This applies to dating too.

Teens are actually sending pictures of themselves in provocative situations to elicit a response. Sometimes it's how they start a hookup conversation. A girl will send a picture of herself in a bikini to elicit a response. A guy will take a picture of himself in front of the mirror with nothing but boxers on. A girl will text back a picture of herself wearing nothing but her underwear, and . . . you get the point.

According to a recent MTV/Associated Press survey, more than 30 percent of teenagers asked had sent a naked picture of themselves to someone else in the last year.[1]

The problems with this kind of communication are severalfold:

1. Teenagers are engaging in what officials refer to as child pornography, and more than one attorney general has looked into prosecuting teenagers for using their cell phones in this manner.
2. Seeing someone without clothes on takes you to an intimate place psychologically.
3. Sexuality becomes the foundation of the relationship before anything else is able to develop.

Our culture is seeing a very dangerous practice become the norm. You must warn your kids before they get involved in the sexting culture. It's extremely dangerous and will turn out to be a generational problem.

I can't overstate this fact. The teens I talk with have been involved or have close friends involved in taking naked pictures of themselves. It's in both public and Christian schools. And it's happening all over the country. You would be wise to keep an eye out for sexting in your neighborhood.

Being friends on Facebook: You might as well.

To date, there are more than 500 million active Facebook users. And that's just Facebook.

Facebook, MySpace, Twitter, and other social-networking sites give us an interesting study of our culture and the value of relationships. Many of these sites have pseudofriendship levels, and you can allow people to see whatever you want them to see about you.

For some reason, these social-networking sites provide a barrier in the minds of teenagers. They think the photos they post will be seen only by those they want to see them. They really believe the notes they post on their wall will be read only by those for whom they are intended. The beauty of this innocent behavior is that you can find out what's really going on behind the scenes if you just take a second and become a user.

I recently interviewed a mother who decided she wanted to peruse her son's Facebook account. She created a profile and asked him to be a friend, and the kid rejected her request. He knew he didn't want Mom sneaking around where he and his friends make crude comments, post filthy photos, and live this secret, seedy life.

So she decided to create another profile.

Now I'm not promoting any sort of deceit here, but I did think this was hilarious.

She Googled the word *teenager* and found a photo of someone online. She didn't know the person. Her son didn't know him. For all practical purposes, this photo was just some random teenager who happened to have a picture on Google images. She changed her Facebook profile to this boy's name and include his picture. When she asked her son to be a "friend," this time he accepted. She had full access to his life. (Now, if you have to go around policing your son or daughter like this, it's imperative that you start depositing meaningful money in your child's bank account today. A lot of damage is done between childhood and adolescence, but it's not too late to make your deposits.)

And I've started using Facebook! We've made it a requirement in our house: If you want a Facebook profile, Mom and Dad have to be on the list of friends. That's just how it is. If our kids don't want a Facebook profile, that's okay with us. It's just good to have open and honest accountability. Not in order to look over someone's shoulder but to help break down the walls of compartmentalization in your teen's life. Facebook has a much more realistic (and safe) feeling if Mom and Dad are there too. There has to be healthy accountability.

Which brings me to the final core value.

4. Be real, flaws and all.

We can't exercise our ability to develop deep relationships if we're hiding things in the corners of our lives. For years, Christians have thought, If *I only show them a good face, they might believe in the God we worship*. But what kind of life is that? Frankly, it's a lie.

Sometimes people feel sad, and it's okay to walk through life and mourn together.

Sometimes people mess up, and it's okay to admit it.

It's okay for people to know you.

It's okay for you to know others.

It's the difference between *being* human and *acting* human.

So, when your teenagers try to play the privacy card or throw out the "You don't trust me!" line, just remember the essence of humanity is knowing each other and being known by each other.

This is probably where I see the biggest failure of parenting or mentoring, and it's an honest mistake. We don't want our kids to know the "old" us. We all have history with dating. We all have stories we'd rather not share in detail, probably because we don't want to give our kids any ideas. Or maybe we see the failure in our own lives, and we don't want our kids to go down the same road. But just because you failed in a certain situation doesn't mean you can't tell them and show them where you're coming from.

If you see a teenager going through a situation you know is going to be harmful, pull them aside and help them to see how that same situation shaped your life. Be transparent about your past. It doesn't mean you have to go into the gory details, but a teen hearing about a personal experience from someone they trust can help them gain a glimpse into the possible future consequences.

Accountability isn't a police force asking the hard questions so you can take someone to the spiritual jailhouse and "book 'em, Danno." Accountability can be as simple as living life together. Show the teen you're willing to be honest. You can help him or her see how the decisions you've made in the past led you to the place you are in life.

My ears start burning when I hear youth leaders trying to be the moral police for the teenagers in their group. Sure, you can share and teach the moral compass of dating, but how much richer might your relationships be if you learned how to trust each other?

The Bible says it like this: "As iron sharpens iron, so one man sharpens another" (Proverbs 27:17).

And contrary to popular belief, it can work.

It can work when there is trust at the core.

It can work when both parties are interested in being the *best* God made us to be.

It can work when both parties are honest.

It can work if we don't use our accountability time to introduce guilt or shame.

But it won't work if you think you're the policeman.

It won't work if your life is dramatically different from the one you claim.

It won't work if there are skeletons in your closet that you're always trying to hide.

However, when you're honest and realistic with teens, it's a great way for your kids to see boundaries and to learn what it means when someone truly loves them, even in the context of dating.

It's okay to have a set time to call home.

It's normal to have people in the community calling to report what they see in public.

Healthy accountability is the difference between allowing our culture to teach teens how to date and taking the bull by the horns and teaching them ourselves.

It takes work.

It takes time.

It takes energy.

It takes initiation.

But the beauty of healthy accountability is the depth of relationship you're going to enjoy. It's going to set your teenager on the right road in terms of dating. And you'll benefit from meeting and knowing your teenager's friends.

Dating is a natural cultural builder. It shouldn't be something to be afraid of; rather, it should be a growth lesson. Teenagers need to know how, what, and when to date. Boys need to know how to talk to girls. Girls need to know they can be friends without marrying.

With a little discussion and a lot of intentionality, dating can be a healthy learning experience, void of sexual immorality.

CHAPTER 7

WHO SHOULD I DATE?

EARLIER I REVEALED a youth leader trick of the trade to get teenagers to start talking about who they want to date. Remember?

"Who do you want to go on a date with?"

And all the boys screamed, "She's gotta be hot!"

As this example clearly shows, it's imperative to set some guidelines for the type of people teenagers should date. Now, be careful: Setting guidelines doesn't mean God is etching the commandments into tablets of stone.

Guidelines are just that: *guidelines.*

They can shift and change.

They can take different form.

They can be made to fit a certain situation.

Guidelines are a starting place.

When I was in high school, I played basketball. I mentioned my coach earlier, as he was a vital mentor in my life. He spent hours helping me understand important life lessons that guide me even to this day.

I remember one game we had my junior year.

We were playing our rival team, and it was the first game of the play-offs. Our small school wasn't known for getting to the play-offs very often, so when the news hit that we were going to make it to the big show, the whole town showed up!

I remember getting to the gym before the game, and people were standing outside trying to get in. *It was packed!*

We started our usual warm-up routine, and it was so exciting that thousands of people were there to cheer us on to the championships.

The whistle blew, and the game began. I was playing a small forward position, intent on making this the best game of my life.

Three minutes into the game, I had shot seven times—and missed all seven.

My coach called a time-out and met me in the middle of the court. "BRANER!" He was not happy. "What are you aiming at?"

Now, I have to stop here for a second and let you know how much I loved basketball. I went to the gym every chance I could. I shot thousands of shots. I spent an incredible amount of time trying to be the best basketball player I could be. So for this coach to question my shooting ability was a bit of an insult.

"Coach, I'm just shooting at the—"

I had no more than got the words out when he screamed in my face, *"Braner, if you aim at nothing, you'll hit it every time.* Get to the end of the bench."

I lowered my head and walked down to the end of the bench in defeat.

This was supposed to be my game.

This was going to be the gate to the championship.

And now I was sitting on the bench, fuming, with seven missed shots to my record.

Thousands of people now knew that I couldn't play in the big game.

It took a few days, but I started thinking about what he said: "If you aim at nothing, you'll hit it every time." And it changed my life.

If you don't have goals or guidelines in your life, then you'll walk through life as a reactionary. You'll ebb and flow with whatever life throws at you. But if you take a second and think about the goals and guidelines you want to happen in your world, you'll at least be aiming for something.

If we walk through life expecting to hit a goal or a target but never have enough forward thinking to know *what* we're aiming at, it only makes sense that we'll not be able to reach that goal.

SETTING GUIDELINES

I'm not suggesting that we come up with a comprehensive list of characteristics that need to be checked off for every possible date to be a valid potential, but it's probably a smart idea for teens to start thinking about this and come up with some priorities.

Maybe your approach is much like mine.

Have the students give you some of the qualities they are looking for in someone they want to spend time with.

Start slowly.

Don't expect much.

Just spend some time talking about what they might be looking for in a potential mate. Separate the girls from the boys and get a large piece of poster board or a large section of butcher paper. Ask questions and write down honest answers.

The danger in making a list is that teens may think they need to impress someone with their ability to create the perfect mate. *Problem!* There's no perfect guy out there. There's no perfect girl out there. We all have faults, whether physical imperfections, emotional baggage, or even quirks that we've acquired over the years.

The other problem with this idea is that once a teen creates a checklist, if someone doesn't meet 100 percent of those requirements, the teen feels he or she is compromising and settling for less than perfect. I've watched college students and young adults throw away potential long-term relationships over something so small and insignificant on "The List." Remind your students that these are simply *guidelines*.

As you begin creating this list in your group, help them see the importance of just taking off from somewhere. And then let the conversation go.

Start simple:

1. What do you like to do?
2. What food do you like?
3. What are your dreams?
4. What qualities are you looking for in a mate?
5. What common interests do you have?

Keep helping them. Maybe mention something like this: "You see, as you begin to answer these questions about yourself, you're going to notice people with similar interests. This isn't to say that if you like to ride bikes, the only girls you'll date are those interested in bicycles. It's just a place to start so you can know yourself and reach out to people with common goals and dreams."

Most guys answer, "I want to date a girl that's super hot!" Well, there's nothing wrong with being attracted to the person you want to date. In fact, I believe it's a necessity.

Remember those people in your life who accused you of being shallow because you wanted to date a girl who looked good? They started telling you, "But what about her personality?" Which is on the right track—we *do* need to be focused on people who are kind, generous, compassionate, and selfless. But if you're not attracted to them, it's not going to last. Physical attraction is an important point, as long as it's not the *only* point.

So as you create this list, shoot for the moon. Brainstorming ideas is easy when you let your mind flow freely.

You'll probably get answers like, "I need a girl that can cook." Or "I need a boy with great abs." Let it go. As teenagers understand they are engaged in an activity that will ultimately help them look for a date, the answers will get more real. Just give it time. Let it go.

Until you feel like the group is winding down.

When you sense the conversation taking a turn, have them look at the list. Have them read it back to you. I've done this exercise thousands of times, and most of the time kids will list the "faith" piece as one of the last qualities they'll look for in a mate—which I find very interesting!

THE FAITH FACTOR

It amazes me the shallowness of teenagers when considering faith issues in their dating lives. Maybe it's because they don't feel like faith is a major part of looking for a date for the prom. Maybe it's because they don't yet understand what it means to live a life of principle. Maybe they don't understand the ramifications of spending their life with someone who doesn't share their ideas about faith. But whatever the reason, I think it's a prime opportunity to show kids how important it is that we search for someone who believes as we believe.

I've heard many youth leaders teach from this verse: "Do not be unequally yoked together with unbelievers" (2 Corinthians 6:14, NKJV). And they will help teens set up a standard of dating only believers, which I think is a good idea!

I was talking with one of our teenagers not long ago. She was telling me how hard it was to grow up in her home. She told me that her mom was a Christian and her dad was a Jew. They loved each other very much, but they were always arguing about how to worship. They would try to use the kids as religious converts either way, and it was super hard for her as she tried to be kind to both.

The idea of not being yoked with unbelievers isn't necessarily a mandate from the Lord to stay out of the lives of all people who don't believe in God. Rather, I choose to see this command as some really helpful advice. God doesn't sit up on the throne mandating rules and regulations for us to try to figure out. In fact, all of God's commands are helpful guidelines, rules that help us to live better lives. He wants us to understand why He created us and how we can live the *best* life He created for us.

Being unequally yoked in a dating relationship is a setup for hard times to come.

It starts innocently enough.

A movie here.

A dinner there.

A ride on the go-karts at the local fun park.

Conversations on the phone.

Homecoming dance.

Prom.

Sadie Hawkins.

And before you know it, feelings begin solidifying for that person. Real feelings. Long-term feelings. After all, if dating doesn't ever have a chance to turn into a long-term relationship, then why are we dating in the first place?

There will come a moment of truth when one person will have to sacrifice for the other. Either the believer will have to conform to the belief system of his date or the other way around. And then it gets really sticky.

As I teach teens about being unequally yoked, I remind them of the conversation they will have to have someday, potentially voiding all the time and energy it took to get to a place of love. If this faith component is at the core of who we are as humans, the idea of sharing life with someone who believes entirely different is incomprehensible.

This doesn't mean we treat nonbelievers like they have the plague. We don't ostracize people just because they don't believe like we do. But we do take a healthy look into the faith practices of those we choose to date so we can be sure to live God's *best!*

CHAPTER 8

WHAT DO YOU DO ON A DATE?

ONE OF THE most exciting parts of teaching teenagers about dating is when I start talking about the practical. Until now, we've been focusing on the theoretical, but what happens when the rubber meets the road, so to speak?

We can teach teens what it means to date.

We can help them understand who they're looking for in a date.

We can even show them God's *best* for them.

But until we get to the *how*, we've just developed a think tank of dating rather than a practical event.

So what should teens do on a date if they get the chance?

Obviously in order to go on a date, they've got to *go* somewhere, right? I mean, sure, it was cute in third grade to write on your notebook paper, "Will you go with me?" and send it to the front of the class to the girl you had your eye on.

Remember when you drew the three boxes and wrote, "Check one please"?

☐ YES
☐ NO
☐ MAYBE

Remember elementary school? We liked to say we were "going together," but no one really went anywhere. It was a casual "How you doing?" on the playground, but it really didn't amount to much.

To date is a verb. It's a commonplace activity in our social makeup that allows us to get to know someone, and conversely for someone to get to know us — but before that can happen, there has to be some interaction.

We all know there can be some radical misinterpretations of what to do on a date.

One high school student told me that dating was reserved for some sort of sexual encounter. "You really only know that someone is dating if they are willing to hook up. Why else would you date?" he said.

I started thinking . . .

I often ask teen boys, "What's the difference between a friend that's a girl and a girlfriend?"

The answers would startle you:

- You can hold your girlfriend's hand.
- You like your girlfriend more.
- You kiss your girlfriend.
- You can make out with your girlfriend.

It is like every high school student thinks dating someone exclusively is a license for physical activity.

Remember, if *dating* is just a word we use to describe some sort of sexual encounter, then we're not really dating. *The Message* translation of Ephesians 5:3 says, "Don't allow love to turn into lust, setting off a downhill slide into sexual promiscuity." Paul was right. When physical touch enters a relationship, everything changes.

Dating can be one of the most useful tools for sharpening a student's social behavior. There comes a time when boys and girls start looking at each other differently. The idea that girls carry cooties usually disappears around twelve to fourteen years old. And if you've ever been around junior high boys, you know the social awkwardness that fills the room as boys try to figure out how to talk to girls.

They make fun of each other in an effort to flirt.

They overdose on cologne that doesn't smell good at all.

They ask their friends to go and tell the girl they "like" them.

But boys who take time to learn how to communicate with girls have a better opportunity to live out real friendships.

Unfortunately, our Western culture is obsessed with physical attraction.

Sexuality sells everything from AXE body spray to Carl's Jr. hamburgers.

So when it's time for teenagers to enter into this cultural dance of relationships, dating becomes everything but what it was intended for.

Dating isn't about using this cultural tool of finding a mate to serve the carnal desires of our hormonally charged physical self. That ceases to be called *dating* by my definition, and I'm certainly not advocating teenage hook-up sessions.

But parents and youth leaders, hear me: If we don't begin teaching our students how to treat each other like human beings, the environment at our schools will only continue to get worse. No matter what I read in the latest news reports, you cannot convince me that teenage sexuality is on the decline. I spend my life with teenagers from all over America, and the explicit stories they are telling me will make the hairs on the back of your neck stand up high.

We must drive home that dating is reserved for a time to really get to know someone. It's a relationship where someone can get to know you. At the end of the day, a relationship where two people can begin to live life together sets us up for a beautiful God-ordained way of "knowing" each other.

It's no accident that He made us the way He did.

He gave us hormones.

He made attraction part of our being.

He invented the beauty of one man and one woman united with each other for life.

So as we teach our students how to react with one another and model for them the ability to develop deep conversations with people of the opposite sex, we *must* help them know what do to.

GROUND RULES

1. What age?

As a youth leader, I get this question from parents all the time. And as we discussed in chapter 3, I try to carve out an average age where everyone can be happy. Of course, kids want to date as soon as they can because it's a status symbol at school. They feel an innate sense of love when someone takes an interest in them that surpasses just a "hey, let's meet on the playground" level. So teenagers are often vying for an age closer to junior high. I'm privy to the conversations on both sides of the argument, and parents often want an answer more consistent with, oh, let's say, *forty*.

So when it comes right down to it, I help parents walk through the pros and cons, and ultimately we find that most kids aren't ready to date until they're at least sixteen, as we discussed in chapter 3. I find that's a good average age everyone can live with. Teenagers understand the logistical problem of picking up a date on a skate-board rather than a car. And most parents see that by the time they're sixteen, kids need to be able to stand up for themselves in a relationship with someone else.

Sixteen is by no means a magical age, and it doesn't bring with it any guarantee of success. But it at least gives us a place to start talking about how, what, and why dating has an important place in our world.

2. Who makes contact first?

This surprises me at every seminar. When we get to the question and answer time, I find that most guys *want* to be the initiator of the relationship. I think that's a biblical perspective, don't you? Most guys tell me when girls call them, Facebook them, text them, or initiate the relationship in any given way, it's a major turnoff.

I think God made us this way. He gave the responsibility of initiation to the men. I certainly don't mean that to sound sexist, chauvinist, or in any way derogatory toward women, but I find that in real-life circumstances, the gentlemen want to reach out and begin the process.

So as we teach our students what it means to begin the delicate dance of dating, we've got to be willing to teach the boys how to approach a young lady. On one of our classic nights at camp, we have an annual country barn dance. It's basically a big party with good, clean fun, and the night is capped off by a real-live dance in a barn built in the early 1900s.

We set up lights.

We play country music.

There's a bonfire outside where kids can hang out.

But ultimately, we want to teach boys how to ask a girl to dance.

Now, you don't have to be a rocket scientist or go to any school-sponsored dance at a public school in America to see that dancing has taken a sexual turn for the worse. Guys pick out a girl and make the school dance something of a sexual encounter with their clothes on. But out here in Colorado, we believe there is a time-honored, respectful way boys can ask girls to dance — and just enjoy each other.

So we teach the guys:

- Approach a girl with respect.
- Ask her if she'd like to dance with you.
- Treat her like a treasure.
- And when you're finished dancing, remember to say thank you, and that it's been a pleasure.

It seems like such a simple teaching time, but when these young men and women return to their schools, they have a higher standard for the guys or girls they want to begin interacting with on a dating level. They don't put up with the common hook-up stuff because they've been exposed to a kind, gentle, fun-filled option. They have a reference point to draw from when it comes to initiating conversation with each other, and that longing for someone to treat them right has become a real-life experience.

THE DATE

After the initiation, it's time to start planning. What should teenagers do when they go out on a date? Where should they go? How can they use their time to the maximum potential?

Where should they go?

Like it or not, most guys today have *no clue* how to take a girl on a date. The only reference points they have are old movies, television shows, pop music, or *maybe* an older brother or sister who has modeled what it means to date in real time.

The other day I asked a group of teenagers, "What would you like to do on a date?" The answers were just as you might predict.

Let's go to the park.

Let's take a walk.

Let's go shopping.

Go to a sporting event.

Go out to eat.

Go play paintball (obviously this was a young man).

Do something active.

Sit and talk.

Go to a school function.

Play golf.

Take them to the youth group at church.

Go see a concert.

Ride go-karts.

What was noticeably missing? *Go to the movies.*

Isn't it interesting that teenagers can sense a problem with going to the movies? They know if you sit in a dark room for two hours, you've wasted an opportunity to get to know someone. They have this intrinsic ability to sense that the ultimate reason for dating is to actually interact rather than to serve their own desires for sitting alone.

I'm fascinated by this.

One way we can teach our kids how to *do* dating is to bring them along. What if youth leaders, parents, grandparents, or guardians carved out some time to share the tradition with teenagers. What if you took a group of kids on a trip to an amusement park or to an event in your town where they can see the mystery of dating unveiled? It doesn't have to be about something physical or romantic; instead, they can watch us model a platonic event with foundations built for relationships.

We can't expect our kids to know what to do on a date if we don't model dating for them.

Moms and Dads, go out and show your teenagers what it means to have a good time.

What do they talk about?

When Jamie Jo and I started dating, it was important for me to know everything I could about her. I wanted to know what she liked, what she didn't like, how she responded to certain situations, and how I could find commonality.

I remember long rides home from college when we played "The Truth Game."

It's simple. No questions are taboo. Nothing is off limits. The single rule in the game is you have to answer *honestly*.

As we came up with really honest questions and began sharing really honest answers, something special started happening. We started really getting to know each other. I knew at any given point if her views didn't line up with mine, we could continue being friends, but I wanted to make sure I knew as much about her as I could during the time we spent together.

Unfortunately, it seems that the ability of kids to communicate today is at an all-time *low*. I've been dealing with teenagers for more than fifteen years, and I'm seeing kids who grew up thinking YouTube has always been around. They don't know a world without MySpace or Facebook. They don't know what it was like to have to talk to someone face-to-face. After all, they can simply text each other back and forth without any risk or consequence of entering into a real conversation.

As we teach our kids to date, let's rekindle the art of conversation. It might be "The Truth Game" or some other silly way of forcing our hand in conversation, but we can begin to turn the tide of dating back to the place it needs to go by simply teaching them how to talk to each other.

What happens when it's over?

This is probably the most awkward part of a date.

What does a guy do when he takes her home?

How do they end a date?

In the movies, a date always ends with a kiss. The good-looking guy walks the sexy girl up to the house, and there's this awkward moment when they don't know what to do. Of course, as we watch the movie, we're rooting for the guy to kiss the girl and wind up happily ever after. But in real life, we need to teach our kids how to end a date well.

When I was in high school, it was the weirdest part of a date to sit outside and wonder, *How do I leave?*

I remember a friend of mine telling me how he committed to staying pure in his dating relationship. He pulled up to his date's house on a warm muggy night in the middle of the summer to drop her off. They committed to "not touching" while they were dating, and that included the goodnight kiss that seems so necessary.

He told me they pulled up to the house, he shut off the car, and they just started talking about life, their relationship, and what they wanted for the future.

Evidently in the course of the conversation, he adjusted his position in the seat, and his knee moved closer to her side of the car. Unknowingly, she did the same, and her knee encroached on the driver's side of the car. Both were wearing shorts, and the inevitable happened: Their bare knees touched.

He said a shock wave of passion coursed through his veins because it was the first time they had even come close to touching each other after a romantic evening. He looked over at his date and with a low guttural tone he said, "*Get out of the car!*"

"What? What did I—?"

"GET OUT OF THE CAR!"

Before she could open the door, he started the engine. She managed to just barely get out of the passenger seat when he peeled out of the driveway and sped down the street.

I asked him why all the drama.

"Andy, it was the spark of physical touch. Even though it was as innocent as our knees touching, something came over me. If she

didn't get out of the car soon, there was going to be some inappropriate things happening that both of us would have regretted."

Can you imagine what it must have been like on their wedding
night?

See, it's not that dating is some cruel exercise to entice teenagers
to a romantic physical relationship. I'm not proposing that we put
teens in a position where they will be tempted to act out on their
God-given, normal hormonal selves. But if we can teach kids the
precious value of getting to know someone outside the boundaries of
a physical relationship, we can set them up for a wonderful, beautiful
future with the mate God designed just for them.

And then we can teach them how valuable it is to share their
sexuality with someone when it counts. The biggest disappointment
in the state of teen dating today isn't the games they're playing with
their bodies or even their minds. It's not the countless number of
teens I counsel through pregnancies. It's not even the risk of disease
they are playing with.

The most disheartening part of teenage dating is their inability
to experience the most valuable relationship they have to offer anyone
else.

When God designed our sexual awareness, He created us in such
a way that we can truly know and be known. Sex isn't something that
was intended to be thrown around to please us in any given situation.
It was created in the beginning to be shared with someone and allevi-
ate the loneliness that exists in our souls. It was a way that God gave
humans to share a beautiful union physically, emotionally, and
spiritually.

But when I hear about hook-up sessions happening in and
around high schools today, it makes me sad that they're missing out
on the *best*!

They're missing out on the awkwardness of asking someone to
spend time together.

They're missing out on the butterflies in their stomach when
they start the evening.

They're missing out on the process of really trying to understand someone who thinks differently.

These are all the *best* parts of being human.

Those of us who have been on dates before and those of us who have vibrant, healthy marriages need to learn how to pass it on to the next generation. We can't just throw boys to the culture and expect them to figure it out. We can't expect girls to know what is appropriate and what isn't without teaching.

Remember the role of the apprentice? We don't have this in our world today.

I did my undergraduate work in theater and the arts. One of my classes was theater history, and it was one of the greatest classes in my program. I remember the day my professor talked about how actors became actors.

They didn't just go audition and try to figure it out.

They didn't show up on set and become superstars.

No, they actually spent some time in an apprentice relationship with one of the greats.

They followed them.

They talked like them.

They acted like them.

And after a preset time period, they would graduate to be an official actor in the community.

If our forefathers saw it necessary to create apprenticeships for professions, why is it any different when we teach students about what to do on a date?

We need to create apprenticeships where kids can see what is appropriate.

We need to give them models they can observe of successful dating couples.

We need to show them how valuable dating can be when we do it right.

Imagine a world where teens don't have to try to figure it out on their own but where mentors, teachers, youth leaders, and parents are able and willing to help the kids see what dating is all about.

They can do it.

They want to do it.

We have a generation of teenagers who are more willing than ever to learn from older generations.

CHAPTER 9

HOW FAR IS TOO FAR?

THE BIG THREE issues teenagers have to deal with are sex, drugs, and rock 'n' roll. It's been that way since before we were kids. And these are the most common issues youth leaders point to when it comes to teenage behavior modification.

"If we could only figure out a way to get kids to stop having sex." I hear youth workers all over the world trying to figure this one out.

"If we could only provide another program where they could choose to stay away from drugs," they spend hours wondering.

"If we could only _____, then they'd live a happy healthy life."

"If they would only 'do the right things,' then their relationships with God could prosper."

But have we ever thought about this from the teen's perspective?

We don't have to travel too far down memory lane to remember our teenage years. Certainly, for many of us, it was a time of confusion, uncertainty, and loneliness. We tried filling our lives with things that mattered, or at least the things that mattered at the time.

If we drank, it wasn't because we liked the taste of alcohol.

If we did drugs, it wasn't because we thought it would be healthy.

If we slept around, it wasn't because we were just carnal humans looking to satisfy urges.

The reason teenagers behave like they do isn't that different from why adults act the way they do. Adults are just better at covering up their dating behavior or finding ways to justify it. Teenagers are in one of the most heightened times of hormonal transition in life. (Okay, a pregnant woman probably deals with more, but sexual awakening is a confusing time.) They begin feeling things they're not used to.

This coming-of-age is being defined by every media outlet around them, and they're looking for someone to stand up and help them navigate these new exciting sensations within them.

Many of us have stepped back and simply said, "Don't have sex till you get married," thinking we're doing God's work. But I'm afraid that turns out to be a confusing message.

One teenage boy put it this way: "Why did God give me all these desires for women and then tell me I can't touch them? Isn't that a cruel and unusual God?"

I'd never really thought of it like that, to be honest.

This particular teen was drawing a picture of a God up in heaven who shoots these intense sexual desires into his soul, and then with one fell swoop says, "Now deny all the urges I give you." Can you imagine trying to serve a God who you think is playing games with your life?

How hard it must be to walk the halls of high school today and be consistent with your faith?

Movies are telling us that in order to be popular, we have to hook up with the girl.

Television is telling us a sexual story, that it doesn't really matter who you sleep with.

Music is filled with erotic lyrics that tell our kids it's okay to go and do whatever makes you feel good.

Teachers are passing out condoms, and churches are unwilling to touch the topic of sex for whatever reason, feeling dirty or unchurch-like.

I see it everywhere I go, and I just thank God that I'm a happily married man. I can't imagine trying to navigate sexuality as a teenager today. So when they come to me looking for answers, I do all I can to help.

Every dating session I facilitate with students comes down to *the* question teenagers are asking: "How far is too far for me to go with my date?" In other words, how far can I go physically with my date and still be under the banner of God's grace?

This is where the topic of dating starts to shift. The controversy around dating, at least in the Christian community, centers around the ability or inability to answer this question. Because if dating is simply a license to have a physical relationship, it only makes sense that we start doing away with the value of dating.

Some popular youth leaders have stepped out on a limb and proposed teenage dating as something we should protest. After all, if kids aren't out dating, how can they get into this physical trouble? So the answer is quickly reduced to kissing dating goodbye.

Other groups try to throw banquets, dating seminars, and other abstinence rallies to get kids to commit to abstinence until they are married. But the truth is, today's teenagers are comfortable sitting in an abstinence session on Friday night and going right back to their hooking-up lifestyle on Saturday night. Remember, it doesn't even faze them.

There are a lot of parents and leaders out there who are quick to point their fingers at kids to accuse, but it doesn't take long to see how the system has been passed on from parent to kid. Ask yourself how consistently you live in your everyday life as it compares to your faith. We try to teach our kids a belief system, but we don't give them the ability to process life when we are unable to live up to our own standards. Unfortunately, we've created a system of rules where our kids are willing to lie about behavior, and in the end, it's our modeling that teaches our kids how to be deceitful and dishonest.

Please know that I'm an advocate for promoting abstinence, but let's be honest: Just putting a purity ring on doesn't curb the problem. We've got to face reality and know what's going on, why it's going on, and how we can begin to communicate real answers to kids who are asking real questions.

As a matter of fact, I find Christian kids are often the worst when it comes to physical relationships because they get so good at hiding their actions from those who would tend to discriminate against them if they only knew what was really going on. They are masters of deceit for fear of being disgraced, and it shows in the way Christian kids are dating.

What we know . . .

Teenagers are more sexually active than ever.

Dating relationships have all but disappeared, and teens have given in to hook-up meetings.

Sexual activity is expected at certain levels of modern dating relationships.

There are a lot of hurting kids out there.

The feelings of guilt, shame, and inadequacy before God are on the rise.

Kids don't know where to turn, so they turn to each other.

What we in the Christian community do well is teach our students that sexual activity is wrong before marriage.

What we've failed to show them is the value of a healthy sexual life in the future.

We've taken a behavior modification stance and turned physical dating relationships into somewhat of a taboo, but we haven't shown them why.

As a result, so many of our kids are trying to figure out the mixed messages they're hearing from pop culture and from friends, only to wind up failing because they have no foundation for the *why*.

Before you even begin on the topic of abstinence, you *must* have already laid a foundation for what teenagers believe about God and humanity around them. It doesn't make sense to simply put rules down and say, "If you do this . . ." We've got to start teaching foundational truths for teenagers so they can begin locking into the fundamental propositions that govern their own sexual maturity.

THREE FOUNDATIONAL TRUTHS
1. God created sex.

It was early in the history of the world that Adam was given the job of naming the animals. I've often said that if I had a chance to make a movie about the beginning of time, I'd love to work on this scene.

Imagine Adam sitting on a stool thinking up all the names of the animals.

Can you see it?

He sits there as God brings the animals by, two by two.

He sees the one with the long trunk for a nose. "Elephant," he says with delight.

The one with geometric shapes on its long neck. "Giraffe," he finally claims with a bit of confidence.

The big one with a large belly hobbles up. "Hippopotamus." And the heavens explode with laughter.

Through all this, Adam notices there are male animals and female animals. He's confused as he looks around and notices two elephants, two giraffes, two hippos, but only one human.

Soon after, God causes Adam to fall into a deep sleep. He takes a rib from the man and creates woman. The Bible says, "For this reason a man will leave his father and mother and be united to his wife, and they will become one flesh" (Genesis 2:24).

It's been God's design from the beginning that sexuality be a part of relationships. It's His design that there be one man and one woman to experience togetherness in total companionship. That's the way it's supposed to be.

But we've distorted beauty.

We don't think of sexuality as something that brings two people together; rather, sexuality is something that is used to please us. Sure, sex is a gift given by God, but the beauty isn't found in the pleasure of sex. The beauty of sexuality is the fact that the Creator of the universe designed it and made it for the union of two people who are willing to commit their everything to one another.

Or what about the teenage couple who really loves each other, has sex, and then tries to reconcile their sexual behavior with their view of God? How does that work?

I had a conversation with a good friend of mine concerning his past divorce. I recently found out he was divorced two times before I met him, and I started asking probing questions to find out what went on. He told me he came from a religious family that believed in God and taught a wonderful Christian worldview to their children.

He started having sex with his girlfriend when they were eighteen years old, and he told me he woke up every night thinking, *I'm going to hell. There's no way around this.*

He loved his girlfriend.

He loved God.

He loved having sex with his girlfriend.

But instead of someone coming alongside and helping him reconcile his faith with his love for his girlfriend, the guilt that came with feeling as though God didn't approve of him was overwhelming. I was so sad to learn of my friend's unfortunate growing-up experience because I know things could have been different for him if only the Christian community were around to help.

2. Within sexuality, there are boundaries.

It's no coincidence that one of the Ten Commandments has to do with sexuality. Remember when God called Moses up to Mount Sinai? (This moment was later captured in the popular film *The Ten Commandments*.) Moses was given the law to designate God's people as different. The Israelites were to live by standards different from those they learned while living under the carnal Egyptian oppression.

Remember?

"Thou shalt not kill" (Exodus 20:13, KJV).

"Thou shalt not steal" (verse 15, KJV).

And "thou shalt not commit adultery" (verse 14, KJV).

God understands the heart of mankind. He knows that we are carnal people living in a sinful world and are tempted to engage in casual sexual behavior. He also knows that adultery confuses the perfect gift created from the beginning.

He's not trying to steal the joy away from people who are interested in having sex. No, the law was given to protect the perfect gift He gave us. He said, "Thou shalt not commit adultery," so that there would be healthy families functioning inside the perfect gift of togetherness introduced all the way back with Adam and Eve.

Jesus went even further when He said, "But I tell you that anyone who looks at a woman lustfully has already committed adultery with her in his heart" (Matthew 5:28).

Again, these boundaries aren't set up to prohibit our sexual awareness; rather, God gave us these boundaries to help us understand the perfect way. He desires that we live in the beauty of His creation, void of all the sin in the world.

But much like C. S. Lewis once wrote,

> We are half-hearted creatures, fooling about with drink and sex and ambition when infinite joy is offered us, like an ignorant child who wants to go on making mud pies in a slum because he cannot imagine what is meant by the offer of a holiday at the sea. We are far too easily pleased.[1]

We've traded in God's ultimate plan for something of a joke, and our teenagers are catching on. They watch the way we play with sexuality, and it's no wonder they treat it as less than sacred. It's really no surprise that the hook-up culture has followed the sexual revolution of the sixties. Kids today have seen the cries for sexual freedom from the generation before them, and they know no self-control.

3. Marriage has to be worth it.

My heart is sad as I see more and more couples in the church ending their relationships in divorce. I know there are extenuating circumstances that cause couples to end things, but for goodness' sake, Christian marriages are now ending on par with secular marriages.

I was in the office with a good friend, a popular Christian psychologist, and he bowed his head after thirty years of marriage counseling and confessed, "Andy, we've lost the battle." The Christian community has succumbed to the pressure of the world, and divorce rates among Christian couples are now rising higher than those of non-Christian marriages. I asked him, "After all these years, after all the family-life seminars, after all the conferences, after all the marriage pledges, *why*?"

And he gave me a few reasons:

1. Christians are marrying only to justify their sexual appetite. We've lost the true art of marriage and the meaning of relationships. We've made such a big deal out of not having sex before we get married that we have twentysomethings getting married in order to check the moral box of marriage and satisfy their desires.
2. Somehow we've allowed this idea that "God wants us to live apart" to enter our discussions. And the God card is used to justify our lack of commitment and sacrifice to each other.

3. Christian culture is usually fifteen to twenty years behind the world. Look at where we've come. Our cultural life has entertained the behaviors of the eighties and nineties. Marriage is becoming more and more of a dating relationship ready to be negotiated at any given hardship.

His conclusions made me sad. I know several students who are walking through the ugly aftermath of their parents' divorce. These are Christian families that boasted strong marriage ties, and now for whatever reason, the parents have broken up and the kids are reeling.

Before we condemn our kids' sexual behavior, we need to ask ourselves, "Are *we* ready to stand up for marriage till death do us part?"

Teenagers are watching.

If marriage is nothing more than an amusement ride to satisfy urges, then how can we rightfully stand before them and demand sexual purity before they are married? It's no accident that we've seen the rise in teen sexuality. They just don't believe marriage is worth it.

As a believer and follower of Jesus, I feel like it's my calling to show students the beauty of love inside the marriage covenant. I believe we have a duty to help show them that love is a sacrifice we show to each other. Sure, sexuality is a part of the marriage relationship, but there's much more to showing students the value of marriage within God's ultimate design.

How far is too far? It's an impossible question to answer without a foundation for something beautiful. We can create checklists and litmus tests for students, but without a solid understanding of why it's important to save sexuality until marriage, it's like trying to fight a hellish flame with a water gun.

So before we go off telling students how to rule their own sexual lives, let's bring back the teaching tools we can use to disciple them. Let's mix our programmatic thinking with solid biblical truth.

They're hungry to know why, and unless we start providing good solid answers, this ship isn't turning any time soon.

THE NEED FOR SOLID SEXUAL EDUCATION

I don't mean that we need some cheesy chart to show diseases and parts of the body like in P. E. class with the head football coach at the helm. No, I'm talking about real sexual education. We need to teach our students what it means to be a sexual being created in God's image, here to live out the wonderful relationships He gave us.

We need to teach them the beauty of sexual encounters.

We need to teach them the dangers of sexual activity.

We need to help them see both parts of sexuality so they will know what to expect before choosing to be sexually active.

Let's be clear: It's not working when we just look at them and say, "Don't." So what would happen if we gave teenagers a fighting chance? Sure, they'll make bad decisions, but they're making bad decisions already—so what do we have to lose?

THE NEED FOR SOLID MENTORSHIP PROGRAMS

We can't let kids flounder around on their own as they try to find out the right way to sexual prudence. I propose that we have solid married couples in the church or youth group hold forums on what to expect sexually.

Women in the church, young girls need to know what you know. They need to know how to prepare for a healthy sexual life with a mate. They need to know your mistakes. They need to know how to treat a date, what to wear on a date, and how to talk to a boy.

Men in the church, boys need you! They need to know how to treat a woman, how to deal with sexual urges as high school students, how to stay clear of pornography, and how to live a healthy sexual life when they get married.

I know it's not an easy topic to cover within the walls of the church, but if we are all sexual creatures created by God, then let's talk about some of the most powerful driving forces in our lives.

THE NEED TO REDEFINE DATING

So, we all agree that dating can't simply be a culture of hooking up. But it also can't be a precursor to parents wanting their kids to get married at sixteen! I've seen so many mothers and fathers fall in love with the date, and it confuses the *whole* situation.

We need to redefine dating as a cultural practice whereby a boy can learn how to communicate with a girl. Where girls can identify traits in guys that she wants or doesn't want for her future mate.

It's not merely sexual.

It's not physical.

Rather, dating needs a face-lift.

THE NEED TO EXPLAIN THE INFLUENCE OF CULTURE

If there's anything I'm called on to talk about the most, it's how Christians can exist in a culture that is so intensely sexual. How can teenagers survive the latest Top 40 music scene, the latest box-office weekend, or the latest sitcom when they get the sex message loud and clear on all fronts?

I've found that if we're willing to talk about where the culture is going, it gives kids a clear choice between the message of the world and the message of God's perfect plan. If we run from the world and try to bury our heads in the sand, the world continues spinning, and we become out of date and out of touch with what kids deal with.

Imagine what it would be like to play a Top 40 song at Sunday school—not so you could have a party, but so you could help kids navigate the opposing messages the world tries to send them.

I once heard a pastor say, "You don't need to study all the counterfeit dollar bills to know what true money looks like. You just need to study the one that is true." And although I understand the point of the argument, I think it falls apart when you're talking about culture. It especially falls apart when you're talking about sexuality in culture.

How often have you taken the time to see what Jesus thinks about sex? Probably not very much. But our culture is inundated with sex. So how do you apply biblical principles written in a culture that didn't have near the sexual influence we have today? It's a tough bill to sell.

American culture is driving our sexual lives right now. Let's step back and help kids see the reason God created sex and how they can be a part of it as they grow into mature adults.

It doesn't take much to begin an honest discussion with the teenagers in your group. They're always readily available to give their opinions, and that's all you need. You don't have to be Dr. Phil, Dr. Laura, or any other Doctor of Love for that matter. An honest look at who we are as humans and how we respond to sexuality is often all we need to help kids understand the significance of sexuality in the confines of a marriage relationship.

CHAPTER 10

COMMUNICATION, ANYONE?

MY FIRST EXPERIENCE with pandemonium concerning teenage dating happened in 2001. I had been working in youth ministry for a couple of years and was noticing some interesting trends with teenage sex played out at school when a mom called me.

"You can't talk about sex at church!" she yelled as soon as I picked up the phone.

"Uh . . . my name is Andy, and you are?" I asked a bit poignantly.

"It doesn't matter. My kids came home and told me you were talking about *sex*." She whispered it this time. "Is that true?"

"Yes, ma'am, we were talking about dating and—" No sooner had the words left my lips than this woman started in on me.

"You can't talk to my fifteen-year-old daughter about sex without letting us know. She's much too innocent, and we've been trying to protect everything she sees . . ." She went on and on for a while longer, but the first part had already thrown me for a loop.

Dear parents,
I totally respect your level of protection for your kids. In fact, for some, I'm in awe of how you've managed to pull it off. But let me be the bearer of bad news: If your kid is fifteen years old, *she knows what's going on.*

Studies are showing sexual activity among eleven- to twelve-year-olds now. The days of Andy Griffith are over. Mayberry has gone by the wayside. And even though we try as hard as we can to protect our kids, we must wake up and realize they are compromising their sexuality for a cheap date. Communication is the KEY!!!

Sincerely,
Andy

Okay, now that's out of the way.

I know it's tough to talk with your kids about sex. Nobody has good stories. In fact, it's just the opposite. What used to be a good laugh in the locker room in high school is now a *great* laugh before Sunday school with thirty- to forty-year-old men.

We all sit around and listen to each other tell of the embarrassment it is to share these truths with our sons. As they share the stories of how they broke the news to their kids, we're partly intrigued, but we're mostly embarrassed for the dad who had to let the cat out of the bag, thinking it might be a little early or a little late.

It's just not enough anymore. We can't simply hand our kids a book, have a birds-and-bees discussion, or even watch a movie about human sexuality. Our kids are being sold sex at every turn. At the movies. On the radio. At sports events. Even at school. We've got to be able to breach this topic, or they'll learn it somewhere else. If your kids are going to live in today's culture, they will be deluged with information about sexuality. We need to be proactive in our approach to counter what the world is telling them.

THREE KEYS TO GOOD COMMUNICATION
1. Put your listener above your own agenda.

Oftentimes we think it's necessary to come up with some cute way to present the sex talk to our kids, but really, all they want to do is talk. They don't want to be the headlines of the local men's Sunday school class. All they want to do is learn from you. So, just trust me on this one: Take your time, listen to where they are, and meet them in the middle.

Too many times we get wrapped up in our presentation, when sometimes all students want to hear is the honest truth. Take some time. Spend quality time with your kids. They'll appreciate your willingness to make it something they can understand.

Also, if you're talking to your kids and they feel valued in this discussion, you're going to have lots of opportunities in the future to hear what's really going on in their hearts concerning sexuality.

2. Say what you mean to say.

I was talking to a buddy the other day who was taking his boy out on a camping trip. This was to be the father/son outing where Dad was going to impart the worldly wisdom of sex to his ten-year-old. He was nervous. The kid didn't know what was about to happen. But they were heading to the wild blue yonder.

After they got the campsite set up, the tent in place, and the sleeping bags all rolled out, the father decided to take the opportunity to sit by the fire and break the ice.

"Son, have you ever wondered where babies come from?"

The son's eyes got wide as he realized it was a trap. "Uh . . . no, Dad. But I don't want to."

And that was it.

That was the culmination of this young boy's sexual talk from his father.

Come on, dads. We can do better than that.

We have to address the topic of anatomy. We need to help our sons understand the differences in men and women. I talk to married couples all the time who tell me they didn't even know the anatomy of their partner until they decided to get married.

One of my most recent conversations was with a twenty-year-old engaged guy who decided to take a Sex and the Body class at college. It was the only way he was going to learn how sexuality was going to play out in his soon-to-be-married life.

Dads, let's talk about body parts.

Let's talk about love.

Let's talk about the funny nuances of getting to know someone.

Let's talk about intimacy with a woman.

Let's help our sons understand the difference between pornography and true sexuality.

Let's say what we mean to say and get on with it.

My buddy didn't want to talk about *babies*. He wanted to help his ten-year-old begin to understand the sexual nature of men and women.

Don't mask your agenda. Say what you mean to say and get it out on the table.

3. Listen well.

Most tragic sex talks end with too much talking and not enough listening. When we talk with our teenagers about their own sexuality, it's important that we listen well.

Use questions like:

- How do kids date at your school?
- What does it mean to hook up?
- Do you know any kids at school who are hooking up?
- What do you think about that?

And let them talk.

Let the stories come freely—without judgment, without advice, and certainly without any personal stories. Just listen closely, and you'll win a key to what's really going on in the heart of your teenager.

I know it's not going to be easy.

I know there are walls built in our culture that keep us from asking honest questions.

But I believe the Enemy has used the veil of silence to keep us from really being able to teach our teenagers the beauty of sexuality. He has built a culture that continues to defame God's ultimate design for sex, and it's time we take it back.

God created the most intimate way we can be together as humans, and we need to take back the purpose. We need to show our kids that explicit solicitation of sex is wrong. It's almost like Satan has turned our culture of sexuality into one big prostitution ring. He doesn't require money, but he does require our soul in exchange for a momentary pleasure experience.

He doesn't tell us the perfect way.

He doesn't give us the option to back out.

He uses the same old lie he used with Eve in the garden. Remember that?

It was the scene in Genesis 3 where all of humanity changed.

The serpent was more crafty than any of the wild animals the Lord God had made. He said to the woman, "Did God really say, 'You must not eat from any tree in the garden'?"

The woman said to the serpent, "We may eat fruit from the trees in the garden, but God did say, 'You must not eat fruit from the tree that is in the middle of the garden, and you must not touch it, or you will die.'"

"You will not surely die," the serpent said to the woman. "For God knows that when you eat of it your eyes will be opened, and you will be like God, knowing good and evil." (verses 1-5)

It was the old lie: You surely won't die.

It's almost like Satan wants to use his same old tricks, and the funny thing is, we're still buying what he's selling.

We're still buying the old line, when all the while our teenagers are walking the streets in spiritual death as they try to make sense of this stuff.

Just yesterday I was talking with another one of my buddies here in Colorado. We were talking about growing up, and I told him I was writing this book on sex and dating for youth leaders.

"Andy, I was so guilty when I was dating my girlfriend. We were having sex—*a lot*—and I just couldn't reconcile the beliefs of my family with the love I had for this girl. It wasn't hurting anyone except me."

There it is.

Satan's old lie. You surely won't die.

When you hear those soft lines enter your head, *run!* Because it always ends up *bad!*

Let's help our kids win this one. Let's be sure we're communicating clearly and concisely as we tell them about the world of sex and dating.

PART III

THE TRAGEDY

(And How to Overcome It)

CHAPTER 11

WHEN THINGS GO WRONG

I RECENTLY SAT with a young girl who told me she made some real dating mistakes. She was so embarrassed. The story is all too familiar.

She came from a Christian home.

Went to a vibrant youth group.

Was totally sold out for the Lord.

Met a guy who gave her the impression of love.

Told her she meant something to him.

So she gave herself away.

With tears in her eyes, she looked at me and asked me if God would ever forgive her for what she had done.

Here it is: The beauty and promise of life more abundantly, yet we have teenagers dying inside as they're trying to figure it out.

I saw another young girl I've been counseling for years.

I met with her at Starbucks to hear a heart-wrenching story.

She was a senior and got pregnant by a boy promising her the world.

She hid the pregnancy from everyone until she had the baby. Then she told her mom.

She is now struggling with the idea that God may never forgive her.

She doesn't know if she loves her boyfriend, but she doesn't want to leave him.

FORGIVENESS

What happens when you do the best you can, but kids end up failing in their sexual commitment to their future mates?

One mom called me and told me her daughter was pregnant.

She used every excuse in the book.

"My daughter isn't ready to be a mother."

"We can't help raise this kid."

"I think it will be better if she just goes to have an abortion."

"Then we can work on the psychology later."

What happens when everything we do leads to answers of compromise? I love the story of the adulteress in John 8. Remember Jesus' reaction to sin?

The teachers of the law and the Pharisees brought in a woman caught in adultery. They made her stand before the group and said to Jesus, "Teacher, this woman was caught in the act of adultery. In the Law Moses commanded us to stone such women. Now what do you say?" They were using this question as a trap, in order to have a basis for accusing him.

But Jesus bent down and started to write on the ground with his finger. When they kept on questioning him, he straightened up and said to them, "If any one of you is without sin, let him be the first to throw a stone at her." Again he stooped down and wrote on the ground.

At this, those who heard began to go away one at a time, the older ones first, until only Jesus was left, with the woman still standing there. Jesus straightened up and asked her, "Woman, where are they? Has no one condemned you?"

"No one, sir," she said.

"Then neither do I condemn you," Jesus declared. "Go now and leave your life of sin." (verses 3-11)

Isn't it interesting? Most of us would expect Jesus to condemn the woman and uphold a sense of justice in the presence of the religious leaders. But He didn't.

He didn't sentence her to death.

He didn't even wonder where the man was.

He didn't hold out for her to accept Him in her heart.

He forgave the young lady before the men, and then said, "Go now and leave your life of sin."

What a story!

The truth of life is that bad stuff happens even with the best of intentions. We can do all we can to keep kids from making poor choices, but sometimes they make mistakes. So do adults. We all make mistakes. We all have issues when life deals us a bad hand. But if we truly follow the teachings of Jesus, we've got to come to grips with the mistake, the sin, and turn around with a heart of forgiveness.

John tells us, "But if we confess our sins to him, he is faithful and just to forgive us our sins and to cleanse us from all wickedness" (1 John 1:9, NLT).

Recently I spoke with a teenage friend of mine. She was so disturbed. "Mr. Braner, can we talk sometime?"

"Sure. What's up?" I was perceptive enough to see something serious was going on.

And then she began. "I've failed. I've failed my parents. I've failed my church. I've failed my friends. I've failed myself. I've failed God."

Through her tears I watched this young lady who had been

broken to the core of who she was. I had an idea what might be going on, but I asked as sensitively as I could, "How have you failed?"

And more tears flowed.

"I've been in a relationship with my boyfriend . . ." And the story rang so loud and so true as I listened to this beautiful young woman confess an inappropriate physical relationship she had with a boy back in her hometown.

It's no secret. When we engage in sin—and we all do (see Romans 3:23)—there is a brokenness that takes place when we recognize it. It's not as though we intentionally set out to disappoint our family, our friends, or God's law, but it happens. No matter the cause. No matter the situation. No matter the particular sin. The sorrow of our sin is accompanied with guilt and shame that is often like the loss of a loved one.

This young woman, in her confession, was displaying the consequences of a broken world. At the time she thought the whole world was crashing down, and she was hanging on by a thread.

She felt she wouldn't be worthy to be a daughter to her family.

She felt she wouldn't be worthy to be a role model to her friends.

She felt she wouldn't be worthy to walk into church and sit there like a "Christian" (whatever that means).

I looked into her tear-filled eyes and tried to speak to her broken spirit.

"You know there's liberation in forgiveness. You don't have to carry this with you."

Tears began to flow again.

I spoke to the hurting heart of this girl and said, "God forgives you."

As I watched the spirit of forgiveness invade her guilt and shame, I saw a weight lifted off this young woman's heart. The pain of unworthiness turned into a restful realization that no matter the sin, no matter the pain, no matter the guilt, *God is in the business of forgiveness.*

The beauty of living in a faith that is about redemption at its core is that guilt and shame don't have to be a part of our everyday lives. Some teenagers are walking around thinking that sexuality outside the context of the teaching of the church immediately condemns them to a life without God's grace. Can you imagine?

Imagine the prostitute in John 8. This woman was torn from the bed of adultery in which she was found. The religious leaders of the day, probably intending to set up Jesus, dragged this woman through the streets to throw her before Jesus the Rabbi.

As the mob jeered, tearing at her clothes, beating against her body, they found the teacher relaxing outside and doing what He did best: teaching others to love God.

"What should we do?" they asked with rocks in their hands and arms half-cocked.

He took a moment.

Drew something in the sand.

And without even validating their claims with a glance, He said it: "If any one of you is without sin, let him be the first to throw a stone at her."

Revolution!

We must be a people ready to embody the heart and mind of Jesus. We must be ready to offer the freedom of forgiveness accompanied by the liberation of one's soul to our teenagers who are actively making mistakes.

It doesn't mean we condone.

It doesn't mean we look the other way.

It doesn't mean their sin doesn't matter.

But the weight and power of forgiveness offered to a heart that is broken is the reason Jesus came to start the revolution in the first place, right?

Some religious leaders I talk to have given up the fight already. They condemn smugly from the air-conditioned sanctuaries in which they preach, and they use the power of manipulation and behavior modification to add to the guilt and shame of someone who truly is acting out his own mistakes. And with a judgmental glance they look deep into the hearts of our teenagers and create a place where these young hearts are certain to feel like failures.

So what happens when they act like humans?

Maybe instead of picking up the rocks to point out the faults of the teenage generation, we need to shore up our hearts with compassion. We need to meet our teenagers where they are. We need to begin to live life on the same plane, without compromising the initial message Jesus had for us.

Sure, the Christian life is supposed to look different.

Our actions should be noticeably different from the world's.

This is exactly why the power of forgiveness given in real time will show the world even more how we embrace the redemptive message that God has for us.

Unfortunately, as a people, we are slow to forgive. We feel like there needs to be consequence for sin and people should endure the penance of choosing not to follow God. But who are we to impose such a judgment?

Our job is to simply and clearly show God's mercy to those who continue to run away from His perfect plan. The Bible is clear when it says, "While we were still sinners, Christ died for us" (Romans 5:8). God didn't withhold His plan of redemption because we indulged in a lifestyle contrary to His creation. He gave us a way—a free way—to experience what a merciful God might do on His terms.

The most powerful way you can show teenagers you care is to live life with them. Show them a heart of love in the midst of their own poor choices. And when it's time for brokenness to happen, you will have established a sense of relationship that will carry over to ultimate healing.

I dare you to forgive.

I dare you to care enough about the heart of our teenagers to give them a chance to release all the pain and guilt of living a life away from God.

As a faith community, we will begin to hear the hearts of students more clearly as we stop holding the strings of perfection and allow them to be human.

Recently I was talking to a large donor of our ministry. She's raised two fine young men of God, and I was asking what her philosophy was on parenting. She told me something quite profound: "If the journey God has my kids on is crooked, damn me for trying to make it straight!"

Did you get that?

The pain and suffering endured by a life in recognition of sin can often be the exact road God wants us to go down. The beauty is that God is there to make the way straight again, anytime we ask.

If you confess your sins, He will forgive you of those sins (see 1 John 1:9). It's why the biblical view is the only view where people can live *free!*

One thing in life is certain: Tragedy will come. It's how we deal with tragedy that separates us from every other worldview on the planet.

Oftentimes I drive down the road and see signs depicting the reality of abortion. I've seen the bloody fetus on the operating table. I've seen the ugly pictures of what happens in the process of abortion. I know the people who put those pictures up, and I truly believe they're fighting for the rights of the unborn. But what do you think a teenager thinks when she drives past those signs and has just come from the abortion clinic?

What do you think happens in the psyche of a young woman who thought she might have been doing the right thing, only to come to grips with the horror of taking another life?

We can't simply present the horror of sexual mistakes and hope they go away. We've got to find it in our heart of hearts to reach out and forgive.

What if we saw signs reaching out to teens as we drove down the road?

What if we offered places where pregnant teens could find a sanctuary of safety and feel the love God offers us despite a life of sin?

Mistakes will happen.

Life will take drastic turns.

Are you ready to reach out without a spirit of judgment but rather a hand of love and compassion?

I work with teenagers all the time who are dealing with guilt, shame, disease, pregnancy, and hurt; all of them are looking for someone to care for them.

In fact, just the other night a young girl stopped me on the way out of our ministry. She was obviously upset, and I asked her if there was anything I could do to help. She looked at me from behind teary eyes and said, "I've never been to a place where people care about me so much. Even though they know how awful my life is, they still reach out to care for me."

I don't know about you, but I want to be known for helping to heal the deep wounds a failed sexual life has inflicted on the heart of a person. I want to reach out and help kids understand how much God loves them in spite of their poor choices.

And then . . .

We can try to disciple them back to the fold.

We can build foundational truth back in their lives.

We can help them to go and sin no more.

But in the meantime, sinners are in need of forgiveness.

Offenders need to sense compassion.

Grace can be a powerful tool in the heart and mind of someone struggling with a mistake they made.

It reminds me of the time we got a call from a girl we contracted to work as a counselor for our ministry. We search the world over for the best college students to come and facilitate our summer camp in southwest Colorado. We travel to several colleges and universities, looking for students who are proficient in the outdoors and love teenagers with a passion.

We've got some pretty high standards, and one of the questions we ask is, "What do you think about premarital sex?"

This young lady gave the perfect answer.

She believed sex was supposed to be reserved for a man and a woman in the context of a marriage relationship. She didn't think teenagers should engage in sexual activity for fear of harmful results. She was right on.

A month before camp season was to begin, we got a call from this girl. She talked to my wife first. "Um, well, I don't think I'm going to make it to work for you guys this year."

"What are you talking about?" my wife asked.

"Well, something has come up. I don't think I'm going to have the energy to be at camp this summer."

"Well, we need you. You signed a contract. We need you to show up this summer," my wife retorted.

"I don't think you understand—"

"No, ma'am, I don't think you understand. You signed a contract and—"

"I'm pregnant."

Silence . . .

Now, my wife had all the authority under heaven and earth to bring down the fury. She could have pulled out her interview form and really put this girl under the lights of deposition.

"Why didn't you . . . ? How could you . . . ? What were you thinking?" All are questions I've heard from parents when they find out their daughter is pregnant and trying to figure out what to do next.

But she didn't go there.

No, she took the high road, and she said, "Well, I guess you won't be coming to camp." And they both laughed. "Well, you know you made a mistake," she continued, "and so as soon as you figure out how to ask forgiveness from God, from the boy, and from your family, let's start a celebration!"

"*What?*" I could hear her on the other line.

"Well, you don't want to live your whole life wondering about a mistake. And you only get one chance to have your first baby. So let's celebrate. If you want to know what's coming at each trimester, I've got a book I'll give you. If you need diapers, we've got plenty. If you need a stroller, we've got three. And if that guy won't show up for the birth of your baby, let me know, and I'll sit with you in the hospital. I'll help walk you through this as much as I know how."

I could hear the girl crying on the other end of the line.

She knew she had made a mistake, and she probably had enough people trying to condemn her for her decision. She needed grace and mercy. She needed someone who would forgive her with no strings attatched. She needed my wife.

And isn't that how it goes?

So often we are free to offer our forgiveness as long as the other person understands how valuable it is. It's almost like you need them to feel how much it costs you in order to feel a bit of relief.

I'm proposing we stop all that.

God doesn't love us only in the good times.

He didn't look down and offer His Son when it was convenient, or when we got it.

No, "while we were still sinners, Christ died for us" (Romans 5:8).

Shouldn't that be the way we treat kids who make mistakes here on this earth too? Let's be known for reaching out to teenage moms rather than condemning a problem they know is wrong already.

CHAPTER 12

ABUSE AND CHEATING

WHEN I POLLED teenagers about how I could help them with dating and sexuality, one of the issues that rose to the top was abuse and cheating. They wanted to talk candidly about the pain caused when someone you care so much for actually lets you down.

How does it work when someone looks you in the face and with all sincerity is able to convince you that they love you more than life itself? And then that same person has the ability to get what they need and then just leave?

Or what about the person who is so controlling they have to tell you what to do and how to do it? I've got a friend who married a controlling man. She loved the idea that someone cared for her enough to help her understand the world around her. She didn't have to think. He told her what to wear, who to hang out with, and how to think. It seemed like a good match. She just let him control her.

What happens when it all ends?

How do we define abuse?

What do we do when the loneliness feels like it's been taken care of, and then all of a sudden we plunge back into the spiraling feeling of solitude?

ABUSE IS ABUSE

According to a special report by the Bureau of Justice:

- About one in three high school students has been or will be involved in an abusive relationship.
- Forty percent of teenage girls, ages fourteen to seventeen, say they know someone their age who has been hit or beaten by a boyfriend.
- In one study, 30 to 50 percent of female high school students reported having already experienced teen dating violence.
- Teen dating violence most often takes place in the home of one of the partners.
- In 1995, 7 percent of all murder victims were young women killed by their boyfriends.
- One in five college females will experience some form of dating violence.
- A survey of 500 young women, ages fifteen to twenty-four, found that 60 percent were currently involved in an ongoing abusive relationship, and all participants had experienced violence in a dating relationship.
- One study found that 38 percent of date rape victims were young women, ages fourteen to seventeen.
- More than half of young women who were raped (68 percent) knew their rapist either as a boyfriend, friend, or casual acquaintance.
- Six out of ten rapes of young women occur in their own home or a friend or relative's home, not in a dark alley.[1]

A young woman came to me about three years ago with a story I could hardly believe. She told me how her high school boyfriend started by writing beautiful love notes. He sent flowers on Friday and made sure she felt like a queen. She was enamored with the attention. Feeling like a princess, she fell in love fast.

But it wasn't long before he was using lines like, "If you love me, you'll sleep with me."

Sex led to more control, and before long she found herself in a physically dangerous situation.

He hit her.

He forced her to act out.

He asked her to serve him with unreasonable requests.

She wanted to leave, but she didn't want to give up on a relationship that had gone so far.

It's the long, hard story of abuse.

I've seen a trend in the last five years in high schools around the country. Physical abuse has turned into something not simply reserved for domestic marriage relationships. Kids are picking up on it, and they're acting out.

It's one thing to talk to our kids about their sexual behavior, but we *must* also make it clear what constitutes abuse. Teens should never feel forced to do something they don't want to do by a boyfriend, girlfriend, or friend, especially something hurtful or detrimental to their health. They should never be forced into a situation that makes them uncomfortable. And if they are, they need to know to just walk away. Being surrounded by people they love and trust will make the walking away a lot easier.

CHEATING IS CHEATING

Another sad development in the teen dating scene is the visible lack of commitment to each other. Remember, I think dating can be used as a tool to get to know one another. It's a cultural tool we can use to identify those characteristics we like in a mate. *But* . . . if commit-ment is a part of entering a relationship, then commitment is something in need of definition.

To be committed to one another is a very dangerous way to date.

As emotions solidify into something that feels safe and secure, the risk of betrayal also increases. This intensity is the reason most Christian organizations are not in favor of teenage dating, and it has often been the reason people use for kids not dating.

"They're only practicing for divorce," a good friend would often say.

And to be honest . . . there's some truth in that.

Divorce rates are continuing to climb in our culture, and I wonder why.

Is it really true that husbands are tired of their wives?

Can it be that the promises people make at the altar are merely ceremonial?

What happened to "till death do us part"?

Cheating in a committed relationship can do severe damage to a teen mind that relies on the confidence and security of relationship.

I was listening to a guy the other day as he explained the ins and outs of his dating relationship.

"We were at a party. She was drinking. Before I knew it, she was dancing with my best friend. Come to find out, they hooked up. It was over."

Can you imagine?

We all know one of the biggest problem in the teen world today is the lack of stable relationships. Parents are divorcing, friends are on the fringe, and *nobody* is a constant. It continues to shoot arrows of loneliness into the hearts of a generation and can be a cause of future trust issues.

I know the fear of rejection.

It's a powerful, driving force.

It turns an optimist into a pessimist.

And it's totally unnecessary.

As we teach our kids how to put real faith in something, it's important that we make sure the stability they long for is found in something that is immovable. They need a constant.

Isn't it interesting that the psalmist wrote, "The LORD is my rock, my fortress and my deliverer; my God is my rock, in whom I take refuge. He is my shield and the horn of my salvation, my stronghold" (Psalm 18:2)?

Dating can't be a substitute for the longing for a stable relationship.

The only real, stable relationship in our world anyway is the one we have with God. People will always let us down, and teenagers are the kings and queens when it comes to hurting each other. Most of the time they don't know what they're doing, but the reality is, teenagers are experiencing the loss of relationships all across the board.

Let's not forget it was God who created us.

He created the stars in the sky.

He created the planets as they spin.

He put into orbit all the celestial beings.

And *He created us!*

The Bible says,

> You created my inmost being;
>> you knit me together in my mother's womb.
> I praise you because I am fearfully and wonderfully made;
>> your works are wonderful,
>> I know that full well.
> My frame was not hidden from you
>> when I was made in the secret place.
> When I was woven together in the depths of the earth,
>> your eyes saw my unformed body.
> All the days ordained for me
>> were written in your book
>> before one of them came to be. (Psalm 139:13-16)

Can you believe it? The concept is nearly impossible to be grasped in its entirety, and it's one of those ideas teenagers need to know. They need to know that God was involved in their lives from the beginning. He says over and over in the Scriptures, "I will never leave you nor forsake you" (Joshua 1:5).

Not only did God see fit to create you, He also saw fit to walk through life *with* you.

It's *the* issue that differentiates the Christian worldview from any other on the planet. No other God decided to come to earth and live life with us. Most other gods dictate and demand something from their followers so they can connect with them. It's what gives me hope in all areas of my life.

I serve a God who is interested in *me*! He wants to know me. He wants to walk with me. He'll never leave me. Even when I fail, even when others fail me, God is always with me.

It's important that through a breakup, an abuse situation, or a cheating issue we continue to remind our kids that God is in the middle of their lives.

As my Buddhist friend says, "Faith is everything about who we are and who we become. It is *the* most important issue in the life of anyone." And I think he's right.

CHAPTER 13

BREAKING UP

A BREAKUP CAN be a turning point in the development of every teenager. They feel like they've truly trusted and committed to someone, and then the day comes to end the relationship.

Some studies show that more than 70 percent of high school relationships end in breakup.

What odds, right?

Next time you talk to a teenager who thinks he or she is ready to marry someone, just remind them the deck is stacked against them. You can't change their mind, but at least you made an effort to warn them of the problems ahead.

And let's not forget that this idea of breaking up gives much fodder to a "no dating in high school" position. Remember, dating isn't just about having a good time. It's not just about having someone on your arm at the prom. It's more than that.

I believe as teens experience breakups, they can find some practical keys to moving forward in future relationships.

1. I believe they'll have a better understanding of who they want as a mate. It's important that we learn from our mistakes. And let's be honest here: Not everyone was made for everyone else. Some people have good chemistry, and

others don't. If we can start helping our teens understand the nature of human relationships on this level, they'll be successful in their schooling, vocations, and their future marriages.

2. They'll be able to work through conflict, come full circle, and see a relationship that is laced with all kinds of high emotions. A break up is a unique time when mentors can help guide teens and students to understand how to navigate those hard feelings that often accompany a relationship bound up with romantic feelings.

3. They will experience struggle that helps them understand the human condition on a different level. If they learn how to care for one another's feeling through a dating/break-up relationship, imagine what might come of teens whose eyes are on humanity as a whole. They'll learn to be some of the most caring people around. But, when left unaddressed, the hurt will turn their hearts into a concrete-like foundation void of the ability to feel as deep the next time.

DATING IS EMOTIONAL

I don't care what the stereotype is. Guys have emotions in the dating game as much as girls do. When teenagers start sharing their lives together, they begin to solidify who they are. It's about being known to someone else—and when this process begins, it's hard to stop.

Girls need to be extra careful.

A good friend of mine is a psychologist. He likens dating to a potter making a clay pot on a wheel. He says when we date, the memories we make and the level of sharing that goes on are like the potter putting clay on the wheel. As he spins the wheel and shapes the pot, we become more and more of who we are. Our lives begin to meld and mold into the shape the potter makes. We're almost finished—all except for the kiln, the stage where the clay is baked into its final form.

When we allow physical touch to enter the relationship, it's as if our pot begins to solidify. Its shape takes form, and the way we treat each other begins to develop expectations. If we're physical with one another at a certain stage, then we'll continue down that road because our relationship has been in the kiln of physical touch.

You can see quite clearly that when a relationship ends in a breakup, it's like a clay pot being shattered on the floor of our lives. We don't know where to go. We don't know what to do. All of our expectations are smashed in one fell swoop. It's a very dangerous time.

DATING IS SPIRITUAL

God made us to be attracted to the opposite sex. In the very beginning when God placed Adam and Eve in the garden, it was a sort of spiritual union. So even though there isn't a reference to dating in the whole Bible, God set up a natural spiritual bond that is extremely unsettling when disturbed.

It's almost like we are going against what God has designed when we commit ourselves to someone for a length of time and then break up. That's why it's so hard in high school and college to figure out how you feel about someone after you break off a relationship. There is tension, and it's not supposed to be that way. As you look for answers, the hurt piles up; very few relationships are able to survive in the friend stage after a severe breakup.

Please discuss the dangers of breaking up at the same time you tackle the topic of dating with your students. Teens need to learn what it is, what it entails, and ultimately how to deal with it.

DATING IS PRACTICE

The correlation between dating and marriage is easy to see. I've made the case that dating is a cultural phenomenon whereby we can learn what we like about potential mates. But the reality is that when a relationship enters that "official" dating cycle, it looks a lot like a marriage.

Guys stay away from other girls.

Girls are dedicated to their date.

Guys send flowers.

They trade love letters.

They take long walks in the park.

They share life together.

So when a dating relationship deteriorates to the point of breaking up, it can be seen as practice for later relationships to come to an end. In other words, breaking up is a precursor to teaching our kids how to deal with the emotions of divorce.

I think this is one of the best arguments for the lack of dating in high school. When we watch our kids getting married and then watch divorce rates skyrocketing, you have to wonder where in the world they get the ideas? How can they go from "being in love" to "being out of love" so quickly?

I've watched some very close friends go through nasty, tragic divorces, and to be fair, some couples needed to be divorced. But some were treating their marriage just like a well-practiced dating relationship. It was like they never intended to be in the relationship long-term from the beginning.

So if dating is merely a breakup-to-breakup event, I would seriously advise against the practice.

We don't need an increased lack of commitment going into adulthood, as more than half of all marriages end in divorce in the United States today.

I know that's a bleak picture.

I know it doesn't seem like dating is worth it at this point.

But let me take you into the realm of God's intent, and maybe we can see how important it is that we learn how to date right.

CHAPTER 14

A BIBLICAL DESIGN

WHAT DOES GOD say about relationships between boys and girls?

It's no surprise: *Dating is nowhere in the Bible!*

Sure, you have glimpses of relationships.

It talks a lot of sexual encounters.

And *maybe* if you stretch a bit, you might see some courtship happening in Song of Solomon.

You can see God's providence through Isaac and Rebekah, Abraham and Sarah, and Mary and Joseph, but you won't find anything like the culture of dating we have in our world today.

So what are we to do?

How can we teach about dating and sexuality without a verse in the Bible?

I've been to the Middle East.

I've seen the culture where Jesus grew up.

Of course, it's Westernized now, but I've lived with people who closely observe the ideals of the first-century Jewish men who wrote the Bible.

Let's just be honest.

Marriages were derived from arrangements between two sets of parents.

They didn't go out to eat.

They didn't go to the movies.

They didn't write notes back and forth to their friends.

No, mothers and fathers decided long before marrying age who was going to be selected for whom.

So to my friends who are trying to literally date biblically, let me just ask, "Who does Mom have picked out for you?"

If we really want to know God's design for dating and marriage relationships, then we have to spend some time focusing on transcultural truth. It's the way of reading the Bible in its intended context and then bringing the truth meant for all time and all cultures over to America.

We must be diligent to understand that the Bible was written to a certain group of people in a certain time. The beauty is that God's truths can apply across the bridges of history. But we must be sure to do our homework.

WHY ONE MAN AND ONE WOMAN?

In a culture having a critical conversation concerning the value and rights of people who are looking to live alternative lifestyles, it's important to see how God designed marriage:

The LORD God caused the man to fall into a deep sleep; and while he was sleeping, he took one of the man's ribs and closed up the place with flesh. Then the LORD God made a woman from the rib he had taken out of the man, and he brought her to the man.

The man said,

"This is now bone of my bones
    and flesh of my flesh;
she shall be called 'woman,'
    for she was taken out of man."

For this reason a man will leave his father and mother and be united to his wife, and they will become one flesh." (Genesis 2:21-24)

God's design from the beginning was one man plus one woman. The plan of Creation was to unite two people of the opposite sex in the same place whereby each could know the other and be known. It is a wonderful, beautiful picture.

Moses wrote it in Genesis. Jesus commented on it in Matthew 19:5. Even Paul repeated it in Ephesians 5:31. It's a transbiblical truth. One man plus one woman is God's ideal team.

FLEE SEXUAL IMMORALITY

We know God intended one man and one woman, but He also set up this idea of sexual purity. In Ephesians Paul wrote, "Among you there must not be even a hint of sexual immorality" (5:3). If we're going to teach a comprehensive Christian worldview, then we must begin helping our kids understand how to steer clear of immorality.

I had a student approach me today. She's involved in the movie industry, and she was going on and on about how on movie sets, there are understood rules about teens hooking up.

She's committed to a one-man-one-woman lifestyle, but can you imagine?

What if you showed up for work every day, and teenage hormones were raging about. In the middle of the hormonal hurricane, a girl walks up and says, "Hey, do you want to have sex tonight?"

How does a teenage boy respond to that?

Paul wrote in 1 Corinthians,

"Everything is permissible for me"—but not everything is beneficial. "Everything is permissible for me"—but I will not be mastered by anything. "Food for the stomach and the stomach for food"—but God will destroy them both. The body is not meant for sexual immorality, but for the Lord, and the

Lord for the body. By his power God raised the Lord from the dead, and he will raise us also. Do you not know that your bodies are members of Christ himself? Shall I then take the members of Christ and unite them with a prostitute? Never! Do you not know that he who unites himself with a prostitute is one with her in body? For it is said, "The two will become one flesh." But he who unites himself with the Lord is one with him in spirit.

Flee from sexual immorality. All other sins a man commits are outside his body, but he who sins sexually sins against his own body. Do you not know that your body is a temple of the Holy Spirit, who is in you, whom you have received from God? You are not your own; you were bought at a price. Therefore honor God with your body. (6:12-20)

The temple argument isn't for drinking or drugs. It's not for music or movies. Paul's argument for keeping our temple clean has to do with sexual purity.

God designed a perfect relationship between a man and a woman, and in its perfection, there are rules for us to live by. As we talk with teenagers about sexuality, it's important that we build a comprehensive view of what actually takes place when they become sexually active. Sex is more than just physical. It's emotional, it's social, it's psychological, but more important than all of those, the idea of God's Spirit living inside us gives sexuality a spiritual component as well.

I wish the teenagers I work with could grasp this concept. I wish they understood the intimacy you can have with a man or woman who you decide will be a sexual partner for life.

So as the culture of hooking up becomes more and more popular, it's imperative that we help students see the nature of their own bodies as they relate to each other. If for no other reason, it's God's perfect design that gives us reason to be people who keep our bodies pure from sexual immorality.

CHAPTER 15

NOW GO DATE!

THE REAL QUESTION then is "how." How can teens go on dates without compromising their moral sexual positions? How can they stay true to God's design for relationships? How can we help develop teens who will grow physically, emotionally, spiritually, and relationally? Yet I still have parents asking, "When is it okay to let my daughter go out on dates?"

Ugghh, we're missing the point.

Sure, there are logistical answers.

I'm sure there are emotional answers.

I'm sure there are even traditional family answers that she was looking for.

But, the bottom line: I believe dating is something that spans a broader topic than what age, when, and how. The details are important, but the concept of dating is something we must help the next generation understand.

Unless, of course, we are willing to go back to the time-honored tradition of arranged marriages—and there are some parents who are ready to take a long leap back in time.

I'm still an advocate for teenagers being able to date.

They can use dating to get to know each other.

They can figure out that men and women think differently.

They can begin to think about what qualities they want in a mate.

They can work through conflict and begin the long process of understanding commitment.

Boys can learn how to treat girls with respect.

Girls can learn how to treat guys.

I believe the Christian worldview allows us to define dating as an exercise in learning to socialize with members of the opposite sex. We have a cultural responsibility to translate God's principles across the bridge of time to make sense of a boy and a girl going out to eat, going to the movies, or even just hanging with each other at a school function.

I don't believe teenagers are just animals serving their deepest desires sexually.

We can guide, direct, and mentor teenagers into healthy relationships where they are able to think about future relationships—mainly marriage—and be well prepared to stand up in any context for foundations of purity.

We can lock arms together and teach boys how to respect girls.

We can give kids hope as they reach out to understand dating in our culture.

We can give teenagers the tools to interpret messages from media telling them to please every desire inside them and then help them make wise, conscious decisions to be in a relationship or not.

If I'm wrong . . .

Then watch dating and sexual activity turn into barbarism and carnal desire.

Watch men continue making women out to be sexual objects of conquest.

Watch as women give in to the "love" factor and continue to accept a life of abuse and being taken advantage of.

WE MUST HELP!

As we begin a journey of education and modeling, we can create disciples of dating.

We can help teens understand the value of their own sexuality.

And, ultimately, we can shine a light on the seedy goings-on in today's high schools — and help turn the tide.

Another student asked me a question: "Do you really think you can change the course of teenage dating?"

I answered, "Remember the story of the young boy and the starfish? The boy walked the beach one day noticing all the starfish had been washed up on the shores of the sea. The tide went out and left hundreds of thousands of starfish there to die in the heat of the sand. The young boy began throwing the starfish back in the sea one by one.

"An adult onlooker happened to be walking down the beach in the other direction, carefully watching this young boy throw each little starfish back in the ocean. 'You know you can't save all these starfish, right?' the adult challenged.

"'Yeah,' the young boy answered. And as he held up another starfish he said, 'But it matters to this one.' And he threw it back in the ocean to live."

We might not see a whole generation turn back to respecting dating and sexuality, but for the one or two who do get it: It matters to them.

NOTES

Chapter 1: Is Dating Even in the Bible?
1. "Divorce and Remarriage: U.S. divorce rates for various faith groups, age groups, & geographic areas," ReligiousTolerance .org, http://www.religioustolerance.org/chr_dira.htm.
2. Debby Herbenick, Michael Reece, Vanessa Schick, Stephanie A. Sanders, Brian Dodge, and J. Dennis Fortenberry, "Sexual Behavior in the United States: Results from a National Probability Sample of Men and Women Ages 14–94," *The Journal of Sexual Medicine* 7, s5 (October 2010): 255–265.

Chapter 4: The New Dating Horizon
1. Facebook Press Room, http://www.facebook.com/press/ info.php?statistics.
2. Andy Braner, *Love This! Learning to Make It a Way of Life, Not Just a Word* (Grand Rapids, MI: Zondervan, 2007).

Chapter 5: Marriage
1. http://smalley.cc.
2. For an excellent resource on expectations in marriage, see Jerusha Clark's book *When I Get Married: Surrendering the*

Fantasy, Embracing the Reality (Colorado Springs, CO: NavPress, 2009).

3. Josh McDowell, conversation with the author.

Chapter 6: Parental Involvement

1. Larry Magid, "Study: 30 Percent of Youths Report Sexting," CBSNews.com, December 3, 2009, http://www.cbsnews.com/stories/2009/12/03/scitech/pcanswer/main5873653.shtml.

Chapter 9: How Far Is Too Far?

1. C. S. Lewis, "The Weight of Glory," *The Weight of Glory and Other Addresses*, ed. W. Hooper (New York: Simon and Schuster, 1996), 25–26.

Chapter 12: Abuse and Cheating

1. Bureau of Justice Special Report: Intimate Partner Violence, May 2000, http://www.acadv.org/dating.html.

ABOUT THE AUTHOR

ANDY BRANER is an ordained minister and the former president of Kanakuk Colorado Kamp in Bayfield, Colorado. Andy's mission is to create a place where teenagers can explore their faith and understand the Christian worldview and to provide opportunities for teenagers to engage in God's work around the world.

Andy recently started a nonprofit camping ministry called Ahava ministries. The first location is called KIVU (www.campkivu.com), and there they provide Christian worldview training to teenagers for fourteen days a term each summer. Andy teaches Christian worldview classes to approximately 1,000 teenagers and 300 college-age counselors each summer. His desire is to teach young people what it means to be "Realife/Realfaith" followers of Jesus.

KIVU has started a gap-year program for high school students to take a year between graduation and their freshman year of college. This program is proving to be a wonderful opportunity for students to explore issues such as poverty and God's view of the poor, international business, and global relationships with different countries. You can learn more about the gap year at www.kivugapyear.com.

In an average year, Andy speaks to more than 80,000 high school and college students in both public and private schools. He teaches on a wide variety of topics, including Christian worldview, basic apologetics, sexuality, culture, Christians in the arts and entertainment, and world religions. He frequently speaks at conferences such as Youth Specialties, Breakforth Canada, and Young Christians Weekend, a festival of 25,000 youth in Branson, Missouri. He has also served as a keynote speaker for the Association of Christian Schools International (ACSI), the Hawaiian Island Ministries conference in Honolulu, and citywide outreach programs for teenagers seeking real answers to hard questions. From 2007 to 2009, Andy worked with Josh McDowell's True Foundations group and Community Core ministry to help students implement relational apologetics.

Andy lives with his wife and five children in Durango, Colorado, where they continue to seek God's will for their family.

More sex education books from NavPress.

How and When to Tell Your Kids About Sex
Stan and Brenna Jones

This book will help you establish a biblical view of sexuality for your kids. Learn how and when to talk with your children about sexual curiosity, physical changes of puberty, dating, chastity, and more.

978-1-60006-017-5

Facing the Facts
Stan and Brenna Jones

Designed for children ages 11–14, *Facing the Facts* equips kids to understand and deal with the changes of puberty. It also examines why God intends sex for marriage, discusses love and dating, and answers tough questions about sexuality.

978-1-60006-015-1

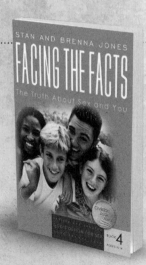

WELCOME TO
KIVU

training global leaders to love God & love others

www.campkivu.com